Portugal

- A  in the text denotes a highly recommended sight
- A complete A–Z of practical information starts on p.149
- Extensive mapping throughout: on cover flaps and in text

Berlitz Publishing Company, Inc.

Princeton Mexico City Dublin Eschborn Singapore

Text: Timothy J. Page
Editors: Christopher Catling, Peter Duncan
Photography: Claude Hüber, Paul Murphy, and Peter Wilson
Layout: Media Content Marketing, Inc.
Cartography: Visual Image

Thanks to the Portuguese National Tourist Office in London and Portugal, especially Pilar Pareira, ENATUR, Turihab and TAP (Air Portugal) for their assistance in the preparation of this guide.

Found an error we should know about? Our editor would be happy to hear from you, and a postcard would do. Although we make every effort to ensure the accuracy of all the information in this book, changes do occur.

Cover Photo: *Pena Palace, Sintra*

ISBN 2-8315-6316-X
Revised 1997 – First Printing October 1997

Printed in Switzerland by Weber SA, Bienne
019/710 REV

CONTENTS

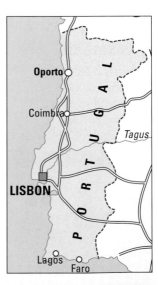

PORTUGAL

PORTUGAL
AND THE PORTUGUESE

Portugal is a very popular destination, though tourists seldom venture beyond the sunny beaches of the Algarve or the lively, sophisticated city life of Lisbon. The country is surprisingly easy to explore, offering a marvellous variety of unspoiled landscapes within relative proximity. Measuring only 92,000 square km (35,500 square miles), Portugal is less than half the area of Britain, roughly the same size as Indiana, and home to a mere 10 million people.

The Algarve in the south, famous for its wonderful climate, beautiful beaches and world-class sports facilities, is only a small part of the whole. North of the Algarve lie the flat agricultural plains of the Alentejo, home to the stunning historical city of Évora. To the west lies Lisbon, a fine example of a planned 18th-century city, rebuilt after the devastating earthquake of 1755. The city sits on the banks of the Tagus, the mighty river that separates the gentle landscape of Estremadura from the bullfighting region of the Ribatejo in the centre of Portugal.

Slightly further north is the varied landscape of the Beiras. Unique ways of life have developed here amongst the seaweed collectors of the coastal lagoons, the shepherds of the mountains, and the students of Coimbra, Portugal's great intellectual centre.

In contrast to much of the country, the far north is distinctly lush and green. Rather than vast agricultural estates, here are small verdant farms and vineyards. The main crops cultivated in the south – olives, cork, oranges and almonds – are replaced by vines, grown in the scenic Douro Valley to provide grapes for the country's centuries-old port-wine trade.

This industry led to the growth of the city of Oporto, situated at the mouth of the great Douro river.

The Minho, north of Oporto, includes the ancient state of Portucale, the base from which the Moors were driven out of Portugal (see p.15), later giving its name to the country as a whole. The region is dotted with historic cities and ancient farmsteads, set alongside pretty rivers that rise in the mountainous national parks.

Isolated in the northeastern corner of the country is perhaps Portugal's most unusual region: Trás-os-Montes (literally 'beyond the mountains'). This is still a land of wolves and witches, where traditional life continues much as it has done for centuries. The region is especially popular with hikers, who come to explore the many beautiful parks, with their isolated villages and dramatic border fortresses.

The Portuguese vary at least as much as their land. The inhabitants of the northern regions show their Germanic and

Today, as in the past, fishing plays a particularly important role in Portuguese society.

Celtic origins in their blue eyes and fair skin, while the dark eyes of the Moors and their plaintive style of singing can still be seen and heard in the south.

The near-continuous round of local festivals and street markets ensures that visitors can experience local life at its most exuberant. Whole villages come to life on such occasions, with everyone taking part, from tiny and adorable children to venerable, elderly grandmothers, dressed in traditional black.

Portugal's long and greatly varied history has left numerous marks on both land and people. The Phoenicians came here to trade, the Romans established roads and cities, the Jews built synagogues and the Moors left great citadels, almond orchards and a taste for sugary sweets. Amazingly, all these strands came together to form one proud people, fiercely jealous of their independence from their encircling neighbour, Spain.

Many Portuguese have emigrated in search of a better life, though a substantial number also return, sooner or later, to the country of their birth. The great 19th-century Portuguese writer, Almeida Garrett, encapsulated the near-mystical relationship the Portuguese keep up with their homeland when he wrote: 'The Italian puts his faith in God, the German in scepticism, the Portuguese in his native land'.

The sea is also a vital part of the national psyche, since fishing provides a living for so many people. Famed for their navigational skills, the Portuguese established one of the greatest of maritime empires. From the 15th century, sturdy ships called caravels ranged over the oceans of the world in search of trading opportunities, and colonies were established in Brazil, Africa, India and the Far East.

As a result, Portuguese remains the seventh most widely spoken language in the world, and the enormous riches derived from the spice trade paid for the country's monumental monasteries and palaces, many adorned with Manueline-style nautical sculptures (see box below) that celebrate life at sea. Long-standing reminders of Portugal's history of exploration are the archipelagos of Madeira and the Azores, situated way out in the Atlantic Ocean. (Only mainland Portugal is covered in this guide; you will find Madeira covered in the separate Berlitz POCKET GUIDE TO MADEIRA.)

Portugal's exceptional climate makes it an ideal location for sports of all kinds. The Atlantic Ocean washes the whole of the western and southern coastline for a distance of 842 kilometres (522 miles). Stunning beaches are to be found all round the coast, not just in the Algarve. Some beaches are long and sandy, and some are tiny cliff-backed coves, but nearly all are great for swimming and windsurfing. Along the west coast are a number of spots offering fine sport fish-

---

Manueline Style

King Manuel I (1495-1521), dubbed 'the Fortunate', ruled during Portugal's Golden Age, when wealth poured in from trade with the Far East and the Americas. The confidence of the age found expression in the architectural style that developed during his reign, which thus came to be called 'Manueline'.

This late-Gothic offshoot is characterized by delicate and intricate carving in stone. Nautical motifs, such as coiled ropes, anchors and exotic plants or animals, betray the inspiration of the sea and foreign lands. The finest examples of Manueline style are all close to Lisbon. They include the Monastery of Jerónimos in Belém (see p.102), the Tower of Belém (see p.102), the window of the Convent of Christ in Tomar (see p.89) and the Unfinished Chapels in Batalha (see p.71).

A religious procession (above); an exuberant Manueline convent window at Tomar (right).

ing and world-class surfing. Land-based sports, in particular tennis and golf, have become a major attraction for visitors, with top-class facilities to be found in the Algarve and near Lisbon.

For the less active, browsing through the many markets for handicrafts may prove more appealing, or simply enjoying Portugal's cheap and abundant food and wine. In either case, the pleasure is sure to be enhanced by the warm, friendly welcome extended by the Portuguese to all who share their passion for their native land. It may not be the biggest or the most consistently spectacular country in the world, but its unique blend of history, landscape and people will ensure a truly memorable visit.

HISTORICAL LANDMARKS

1st millen. BC	Celts move into northern Portugal.
c. 210BC	Rome moves into Iberia after defeat of Carthage.
after AD406	Germanic invasions. Visigoths rule peninsula.
711-18	Moors invade and rule nearly all of Iberia.
c. 850	Al-Gharb becomes a separate kingdom.
9th century	Territory of Portucale takes shape between Douro and Minho rivers.
1139-47	Afonso Henriques (first 'king') captures Lisbon.
1249	Christian Reconquest complete in Portugal.
1383	House of Aviz founded by João I.
1415-60	Discoveries under Henry the Navigator encouraged by his Sagres School of Navigation.
1495-1521	Manueline Golden Age; Vasco da Gama sails for India (1497); Cabral discovers Brazil (1500).
1531	João III invites Holy Inquisition to Portugal.
1578	Death of King Sebastião at Alcácer-Quibir leads to Spain claiming the Portuguese throne.
1640	Restoration of Portuguese independence as João IV of the House of Bragança becomes king.
1706-50	Copious gold and diamonds mined in Brazil.
1755	Great Earthquake leads to Pombal's dictatorship.
1807-11	French invade and royal family flees to Brazil; French beaten with British help.
1821	João VI returns from Brazil after insurrection.
1908	Assassination of Carlos I and his eldest son.
1910	Monarchy ended by Republican revolt.
1926-74	Military revolt; Dr Salazar's 'New State'.
1974	'New State' toppled by 'Carnation Revolution'; democracy established.
1986	Portugal enters the European Union; Mario Soares elected president.

A BRIEF HISTORY

The early history of Portugal is closely related to that of the whole Iberian peninsula. Prehistoric culture flourished first in the north and the Alentejo. When Celtic peoples crossed the Pyrenees in the first millennium bc, they intermarried with the existing Iberian population and built a series of hilltop forts or *citânias* (the best example is at Briteiros – see p.31). The south was visited by a number of peoples who came to trade, including the Phoenicians, the Mycenaean Greeks and the Carthaginians. The Phoenicians established a trading post at Lisbon, and the Carthaginians, under Hannibal, recruited locals to fight as mercenaries against Rome.

Despite the early success of Hannibal, the Romans eventually defeated the Carthaginians and invaded the Iberian peninsula. They were fiercely opposed by a confederation of Celts, known as the Lusitani, living in central Portugal. The Lusitanian leader, Viriathus, kept the Roman forces at bay until he was assassinated in 139bc. Julius Caesar founded many cities, including Ebora (Évora), where the remains of a Roman temple survive (see p.104), and Pax Julia (Beja).

Évora's Roman temple is the best preserved in the country, still standing after so many centuries.

Of the Roman infrastructure, much has survived, including roads and bridges, and the enormous *latifúndia* agricultural estates of the Alentejo, which were once farmed as imperial estates. Here the Romans introduced crops such as olives, grapes and wheat. They also left a strong base of Christian belief and the Latin language from which Portuguese is directly derived.

Rome's decline led to the collapse of the Rhine frontier in AD406, letting in wave after wave of Germanic invaders, who swept across the Pyrenees to sack the wealthy towns. The Vandals passed through briefly on their way to Africa, but the Suevi (or Swabians) decided to settle in the north of Lusitania, becoming Christians. By 585 their kingdom had been incorporated into that of the Visigoths, who ruled the peninsula from Toledo (Spain).

The Moors and the Reconquest

The Visigoths elected their monarchs, a practice that inevitably led to disputes. During one of these, an aggrieved claimant made the unwise decision to invite over an army of North African Moors to fight for him. The Moors quickly disposed of the Visigoths and went on to dominate the entire peninsula, except for the little Christian kingdom of Asturias in northern Spain, from where the Reconquest (*Reconquista*) of Iberia later began.

Deterred by the cold winter climate, the Moors failed to penetrate much further north than Aveiro in Portugal. Instead they settled in the Alentejo, along the Tagus river, and in the Algarve (which they named *al-Gharb*, the 'Western Land'). By the mid-9th century, al-Gharb had become a Moorish kingdom, with a capital at Chelb (Silves, see p.121).

The Moors introduced new crops, including oranges and rice. Their highly distinctive whitewashed houses and filigree chimneys remain popular to this day, as do *azulejo* tiles. Many Moorish place names survive, including that of Fáti-

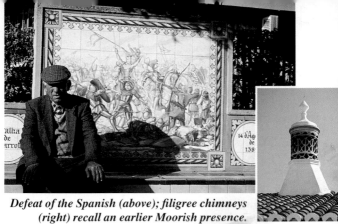

*Defeat of the Spanish (above); filigree chimneys
(right) recall an earlier Moorish presence.*

ma, the pre-eminent Catholic site in Portugal. Unlike their
successors, the Moors were tolerant of the many different
peoples who lived together in Portugal, including Berbers,
Arabs, Christians and Jews.

Even so, the Moors were regarded as an occupying power
by the local Christian population, who sought to drive them
out of their land. The Christian Reconquest was under way
in the north by the 9th century. By the 11th century, Portucale (whose name derives from the Roman cities of Portus
and Calus) had been established as an independent state, free
from Moorish influence and ruled by a count, appointed by
the king of neighbouring Léon.

In 1128, Afonso Henriques became Count of Portucale –
though after his victory over the Moors at Ourique in 1139,
he styled himself King of Portucale. With the assistance of
crusaders on their way to the Holy Land, Afonso Henriques
captured Lisbon's Castelo de São Jorge (see p.94) in 1147.

By 1185 the frontier between Christianity and Islam had
been drawn at the Tagus. For the next 65 years, the fortunes

of the Portuguese varied as they slowly pushed south across the Alentejo, led by Portugal's version of the Spanish El Cid, the heroic Geraldo 'sem Pavor' ('the Fearless'). Not until 1249 did Afonso III complete the Reconquest and secure borders for Portugal (a full 250 years before the Spanish could do the same).

Consolidation

Afonso III moved his capital from Coimbra to Lisbon in 1260, six years after he had called the first *Cortes* (parliament) in Leiria, to which commoners (as well as the clergy and nobility) were invited. His successor, Dom Dinis (1279-1325), consolidated Portugal's borders by constructing castles along the frontier with Castile (Spain). He reformed agriculture and established the country's first university at Lisbon (later transferred to Coimbra – see p.65). He also curbed the power of the Knights Templar, the religious order that had played such a large role in the Reconquest. Refounded as the Order of Christ, and based at Tomar (see p.89), they became responsible to the monarch instead of to the pope.

The last of the Afonsin dynasty, King Fernando I (1367-83), formed an alliance with the English, to whom he appealed for help in his disputes with Spain. When he died without an heir, the Spanish claimed the throne through a web of intermarriages between the two royal houses. They were backed by the Portuguese aristocrats, who were eager to avoid war. Those opposed to Spain (including many merchants) chose João, Master of Aviz, as their champion, and this was confirmed by his victory at Aljubarrota in 1385. Batalha Abbey (see p.71) was built in gratitude. The Aviz dynasty cemented the English alliance by João's marriage to Philippa of Lancaster, daughter of John of Gaunt, in 1387.

Centre of the World

Since Portugal faced the Atlantic, rather than the Mediterranean, where most of the trade routes were concentrated, the country was regarded as being out on a limb. This proved to be something of an advantage when, in the 15th century, the Ottoman Turks came to dominate the Mediterranean. Then, as shipbuilding technology improved, longer Atlantic journeys became a serious prospect.

Peace with Spain in 1411 allowed Portugal to look for conquests overseas. Following in the tradition of the Reconquest, the Moors were chosen as a target. João captured the Moroccan port of Ceuta (to this day in Iberian hands). He was accompanied by Henry, his third son (later dubbed 'the Navigator'), who marvelled at the great riches on offer.

This expedition fired his desire for discovery and he used his position as Grand Master of the Order of Christ to found a

The Moorish castle in Sintra is overlooked by the romantic Pena Palace folly.

Henry the Navigator takes pride of place in the Discoveries Monument at Belém.

school of navigation on the peninsula at Sagres in the Algarve (see p.124), then considered the end of the world. Here the arts of mapmaking, navigation and shipbuilding were improved, and expeditions set sail, in newly developed caravels, to lay claim to Madeira in 1419 and the Azores in 1427. From here the Portuguese also headed down the west coast of Africa, going beyond Cape Bojador in 1434, a feat once thought impossible.

Henry died in 1460, but the voyages of discovery continued. In 1487, Bartolomeu Dias rounded Southern Africa at Cabo da Boa Esperança (the Cape of Good Hope), opening the way for Vasco da Gama to sail all the way to India in 1497-98. This laid the foundations for the lucrative Indian spice trade, previously dominated by Venetian merchants trading with Muslim counterparts and importing spices to Europe overland through the Middle East. Vasco da Gama's feat was immortalised in *The Lusiads* (1572), the epic poem by Portugal's national poet, Luís de Camões (1524-80).

The Spanish were not far behind in the discovery stakes, though the Portuguese claim that Columbus was inspired to make his famous voyage in 1492 by stories he heard from Portuguese fisherman who had sailed as far as the Americas. In any event, the two Iberian seaborne powers agreed to divide the world between them by means of the 1494 Treaty of Tordesillas. This accorded everything lying more than 370 leagues west of the Cape Verde Islands to Spain, while everything lying to the east went to Portugal, thus giving Portugal a free hand in the Orient. Six years later, Portugal also gained control of Brazil, following its 'discovery' by Pedro Álvares Cabral.

The rulers of Portugal, who sponsored these early voyages of discovery, received one fifth of the profits. This 'royal fifth' made Manuel I (1495-1521), the fortunate ruler of the time (see p.10), the richest king in Europe. Trading posts were set up all along the west and east coasts of Africa, in the Middle East (Hormuz), southern India (Goa), Malaysia (Malacca), and even in China (Macau). Profits came from trading in eastern spices, silk and porcelain, African gold and

---

Portugal's Marco Polo

Fernão Mendes Pinto (1510-83) stands out as a true representative of Portugal's early experience of the Orient. He was born in Montemor-o-Velho, 28km (17 miles) west of Coimbra, and embarked on a voyage to the Portuguese possession of Goa, in India, to make his fortune. For the next 21 years, he ranged through East Africa, India, Southeast Asia and China. He was one of the first Europeans to reach Marco Polo's 'Cipangu' (Japan).

Pinto worked as a merchant, pirate and mercenary, and even as a Jesuit ambassador. He made fortunes only to lose them again. The first English translation of his book describes how 'he five times suffered shipwreck, was sixteen times sold, and thirteen times made a slave', and he even resorted to cannibalism to survive one shipwreck.

Pinto finally returned to Portugal in 1558 to write his massive autobiography, *Peregrination*, which seemed so fantastical that he became famed as a great liar, just like Marco Polo before him. Also like Polo, the truth of what he had written was later confirmed by subsequent travellers.

Lisbon's fine Madre de Deus Convent contains a fascinating azulejo museum.

slaves, and through importing sugar from Brazil and São Tomé.

This wealth helped to disguise inherent weaknesses in the Portuguese state. Little of the riches trickled down to the ordinary Portuguese, and Portugal remained a backward place. A great deal of money and manpower was also consumed in protecting the long line of communications to the colonies, and it was not long before other nations, such as the English and the Dutch, began challenging the Portuguese monopoly on the spice trade, so that revenues fell.

No entrepreneurial class developed, as it did in Holland and England. The only real entrepreneurs were the Jews, and they were expelled in 1496 to appease the Catholic rulers of Spain (see box opposite). The Inquisition took root in the 1530s, and the Counter-Reformationary Jesuit order gained control of education in Portugal during the 1560s.

Problems really came to a head when the young and foolish King Sebastião (1557-78) embarked on a new crusade against the Moors in Morocco. His sizeable but very poorly trained army was annihilated in the desert at Alcácer-Quibir, where he and the rest of the Portuguese nobility perished. Sebastião's great uncle, Cardinal Henrique, then assumed the throne, but, being celibate, died heirless in 1580. This precipitated a succession crisis like that of 1383. Philip II of Spain claimed the throne as a descendant of João III, and he was backed by wealthy Portuguese as an alternative to war.

Spanish Rule and Restoration

Philip II of Spain became Filipe I of Portugal in 1581. In the short term, Portugal benefitted from the association with Spain, and Philip upheld Portuguese autonomy, making no

The Jews in Portugal

In the Middle Ages, Jews formed an important and skilled sector of the Portuguese population, working as physicians, tax collectors, merchants, and map-makers (and thus greatly helping Henry the Navigator). They were better treated in Portugal than in many other countries, and some 60,000 Jews escaped to Portugal in 1492 when they were expelled from Spain by the Catholic monarchs, Ferdinand and Isabella.

In 1495, however, King Manuel sought the hand of Princess Isabella of Spain. One condition of the marriage was a crackdown on the Jews. Many sought exile, fleeing to Amsterdam and London; others decided to be baptized and become 'New Christians', whilst practising their Jewish faith in secret.

This lasted until the pious King João III invited the Holy Inquisition to Portugal in 1531. The Inquisitors imprisoned, tortured and killed many thousands of New Christians, and persecution increased under Spanish rule, from 1581 to 1640. Many fled overseas (some to form New York's first Jewish community) and Portugal was rapidly drained of her commercial expertise.

Most of the remaining New Christians were absorbed, but certain pockets of so-called *marranos* continued to practise the basic elements of Judaism in secret, the best known community being at Belmonte.

attempt to unite his two kingdoms. His successors, ruling from Madrid, were not so sensitive and allowed Spaniards to take Portuguese posts. Spanish domination played havoc with Portugal's empire, gaining her the enmity of both the English and Dutch (and their respective East India trading companies). Many ships outfitted in Portugal went down with the Spanish Armada, defeated by Sir Francis Drake in 1588. The Dutch were even more punitive, taking part of northern Brazil and Angola and coming to dominate the East Indies trade in spice. This embittered the Portuguese, many of whom chose to believe that Sebastião had survived the slaughter in the desert and would return.

Spanish rule came to an end when Philip IV (Filipe III of Portugal) tried to deploy Portuguese troops against Catalunya, another rebellious area of his kingdom, in 1640. This led to a successful revolt that installed João IV, of the rich Bragança family, as reluctant monarch of Portugal.

The Portuguese soon mended their fences with the Dutch and renewed their friendship with the English through the marriage of João's daughter, Catherine, to King Charles II of England. This alliance was strengthened by the Treaty of Methuen (1703), which gave English merchants pride of place in Lisbon, allowing for the import of English textiles on preferential terms, in return for concessions on port-wine exports to England.

Portugal contributed troops to the Anglo-Austrian side in the War of the Spanish Succession (1701-13), paid for by fortuitous gold and diamond discoveries in Minas Gerais, in Brazil. Much of this wealth was squandered by the extravagant João V (1706-50) on building the enormous convent at Mafra (see p.83). Convents seemed to have occupied a special place in his heart, as he fathered three children by the nuns of Odivelas!

Earthquake, Pombal and Napoleon

João's son, José, appointed Sebastião José de Carvalho e Melo (later the 1st Marquês de Pombal) as his chief minister in 1750. Soon after the Great Earthquake of All Saints' Day, 1755, Pombal came to dominate Portugal as an 'enlightened despot', and organized the rebuilding of Lisbon.

Pombal showed his power by banishing the Jesuits and executing certain members of the nobility who may have been involved in an assassination attempt on the king. He abolished slavery, reformed education and set up numerous companies to improve and diversify Portuguese trade. Although he lost power shortly after José's death in 1777, many of his reforms survived, laying the foundation for the modern Portuguese state.

Portugal's close association with Britain brought her into conflict with Napoleon when he demanded that Portuguese

Portugal's principal city has a host of art galleries and museums to be explored.

ports be closed to British shipping. France invaded in 1807 when Portugal refused to do this. The royal family fled to Brazil aboard a British ship and the British general, Arthur Wellesley (later the Duke of Wellington), countered the invasions. The final battle came in 1810-11, when the French, unable to pass the huge fortifications at Torres Vedras (see p.85), retreated back to Spain.

The Fall of the Monarchy

In 1814 Portugal made peace with France. However, problems continued to beset her. The royal family remained in Brazil, which was raised to the status of a full kingdom on a par with Portugal, in 1815. Portugal itself was virtually ruled as a British protectorate by the respected, but little-loved, Marshal Beresford. He was ousted by a military coup in 1820, while he was absent in Brazil. This finally persuaded João VI to come back to Portugal in 1821 and agree to a new constitution.

The stage was set for the 'War of the Brothers' between João's liberal son, Pedro IV (emperor of a now-independent Brazil), and his younger brother, Miguel. Miguel suspended the constitution and declared himself King of Portugal with absolute powers. Pedro was thus forced to leave Brazil and fight a civil war to regain the throne on behalf of his daughter, Maria. Infighting continued after Pedro's death in 1834, between those who preferred the radical constitution of 1822 and supporters of the milder 1826 Charter.

Stable government was rare in Portugal at this time and, despite attempts to modernize the economy, the country grew poorer because of the cost of maintaining its colonies. Further problems arose in colonial disputes with the British, Germans and Belgians, eventually resulting in the ignominious withdrawal by the Portuguese from Zimbabwe and Zambia.

All this served to foster discontent. Republican idealists led a failed coup in 1891. The government went so far as to declare itself bankrupt in 1892 and emigration reached appalling levels. Finally, in 1908, King Carlos and his eldest son, Luís Filipe, were assassinated as they rode in an open carriage through the Praça do Comércio (see

The Marquês de Pombal forever surveys the capital from his lofty perch.

p.98) in Lisbon. The younger son survived to become King Manuel II, but he was deposed merely two years later and forced to flee to Britain, thus ending over 750 years of monarchy.

The Republic and the New State

The new republic was unable to provide the stability Portugal so badly needed. Governments changed no less than 45 times between 1910 and 1926, and the country's disastrous involvement in the First World War led to economic chaos. Change came in 1926 when the army seized control. General Óscar Carmona became president and called on a quiet economics professor from Coimbra University, Antonio de Oliveira Salazar, to take control of the Ministry of Finance.

Salazar soon began to produce budgetary surpluses and this enabled him to win further powers. Like Pombal before him, he embarked on a wide-ranging programme of reform throughout education, industry and transport, all designed to bring about his dream of the *Estado Novo* ('New State'). He managed to keep Portugal neutral during both the Spanish

Civil War and the Second World War, allowing Britain to use the Azores as a base on the one hand, while selling tungsten to Nazi Germany on the other. He enforced strict censorship, upheld by the PIDE secret police, and did not tolerate dissent in any form.

To the Present

Salazar's 'New State' began to unravel when Portugal's former colonies started demanding independence, Goa was lost to India, and the country embarked on several extremely expensive colonial wars in Africa. Salazar himself suffered a stroke in 1968 and control passed to his successor, Marcelo Caetano. In 1973, a group of young officers, fed up with the fruitless African wars, founded the *Movimento das Forças Armadas* (the Armed Forces Movement, or MFA). In 1974, MFA soldiers, carrying red carnations in their rifle barrels, successfully deposed the government in a peaceful coup that came to be known as the 'Carnation Revolution'.

After the coup, the Portuguese quickly withdrew from Guinea-Bissau, Mozambique, Angola, and East Timor. One result was a tidal wave of *retornados* seeking to settle in Portugal. Since then the country has fluctuated politically between left and right, but stable democracy has taken hold, strengthened by Portugal's acceptance as a member of the European Union (EU) in 1986, the year in which the respected Socialist, Mario Soares, was elected president. Membership of the EU has brought Portugal into the European mainstream (Lisbon was the European City of Culture in 1994) and it has benefitted from the flow of economic aid from richer EU member countries. Portugal has recently enjoyed high rates of growth, backed up by a strong tourist industry, and looks forward to hosting many more visitors in the build-up to Lisbon's 1998 World Expo.

WHERE TO GO

Portugal's environment varies dramatically for such a small country. This guide starts in the green north (the Minho), and heads south, looking at each of the traditional regions in turn.

THE MINHO

The lush northwestern province of the Minho is one of the most beautiful regions of Portugal. The colour green is much in evidence here, with the Minho justly renowned for its *vinho verde* ('green wine') and for its fine Costa Verde (Green Coast).

The River Lima links a string of particularly attractive towns, such as Ponte de Barca.

This land of vineyards and forests was where Portugal began. It was taken back from the Moors early in the Christian Reconquest, and became the independent state of Portucale (covering an area from the Douro to the River Minho); in 1139 Afonso Henriques declared himself the first king at Guimarães. Numerous splendid monuments survive in both Guimarães and the other beautiful historic city of Braga. Not surprisingly, the region's long history has left its people with a noticeable streak of conservatism, closely guarding the Portuguese character.

The coastline here is blessed with many beautiful beaches, as well as the wonderful resort area around Viana do Castelo. The scenic river valleys of the Minho and the Lima are also unbelievably unspoiled. Further to the east, the Peneda-Gerês National Park is one of Portugal's finest.

Between all these sights you'll discover a highly populated and intensively cultivated land of small agricultural holdings (*minifúndios*), which date back to the time of the 5th-century Suevi (Swabians) and now abound with grapevines. Forests are common, many planted with menthol-scented eucalyptus trees, grown now for the paper trade.

Portugal still has a large rural community.

While travelling the region, you'll notice many partly constructed houses. These belong to the legion of emigrants who presently work outside the country (often in France) to fund a better life back home. They come here in droves for the holiday month of August, and eventually mean to return to the appropriately named Minho (from Minha Terra, or 'My Land') to bask in a much-deserved retirement.

☛ Guimarães

A large sign in the centre of town declares 'Aqui Nasceu Portugal' ('Portugal was born here'), recalling the exploits of Afonso Henriques (see p.15), the first King of Portugal, who lived in **Guimarães** (49km/30 miles northeast of Oporto), before transferring the early capital to Coimbra.

PORTUGUESE HIGHLIGHTS

Guimarães and Braga (*Minho*): historic cities of the southern Minho. Guimarães (see p.28) is the birthplace of Portugal, and Braga (see p.32) is the old religious centre. In between is the large Celtic site of Briteiros (see p.31).

Lima Valley (*Minho*): scenic valley that runs from the wild Peneda-Gerês National Park (see p.37) through the gentle landscapes around Ponte de Lima (see p.37) and on to the historic beach resort of Viana do Castelo (see p.35).

The Douro Valley: the long snaking River Douro runs from the dramatic gorge at Miranda do Douro (see p.60) through the vineyards of Portugal's port-wine country (see p.51) to the beautiful city of Oporto (see p.42).

Bragança (*Trás-os-Montes*): isolated city (see p.58) with a lovely citadel, near to the Serra de Montesinho (see p.60).

Coimbra (*Beiras*): the hilltop university city (see p.64), above the River Mondego, is famous for its varied architecture and good museums. Nearby are Portugal's finest Roman ruins, at Conimbriga (see p.68), and the Forest of Buçaco (see p.69).

Serra da Estrêla (*Beiras*): mountain scenery, and the country's highest peaks, with hiking, skiing and historic castles (see p.75).

Óbidos (*Estremadura*): enchanting walled town, known as the 'Wedding City', with a castle and many small streets to explore (see p.85), close to the historic Alcobaça Abbey (see p.87) and the Monastery of Batalha (see p.71).

Sintra (*Estremadura*): famous town of green hills, palaces and a Moorish castle. Easy access from Lisbon (see p.80).

The Alfama (*Lisbon*): tangle of alleyways, squares and staircases evoking the Moorish heritage of Lisbon's oldest area (see p.91).

Évora (*Alentejo*): designated a UNESCO World Heritage Site (see p.104), with prehistoric remains nearby (see p.107).

Lagos (*Algarve*): lively resort, with old town (see p.122) and beaches running to the dramatic peninsula of Sagres (see p.124).

The well-preserved town of Guimarães boasts a number of beautiful medieval squares.

The city's compact yet sturdy 10th-century castle seems almost to have grown out of its rocky hillock. Seven towers protect a large central keep, lined with unusual triangular battlements that look like serrated teeth. Afonso is said to have been born in the castle and baptized nearby, in the small Romanesque **Chapel of São Miguel.**

Just down the hill is the massive **Paço dos Duques** (Ducal Palace), looking like a mix between a French château and a crusader castle. It was once home to the Dukes of Bragança, but it fell into disrepair and was reconstructed from a ruin in the 1930s. Experts say the reconstruction is not historically accurate, but the 45-minute tour of the interior is interesting for the large collection of antiques.

The historic city centre runs down the hill from the castle along the Rua de Santa Maria to a series of beautiful medieval squares, surrounded by old townhouses. The triangular **Largo de Santiago** is flanked by the arcaded 14th- century Old Town Hall, and a series of townhouses converted into a pousada (p.178).

Through the arcades is the central Largo da Oliveira, where the excellent **Alberto Sampaio Museum** is located in the Collegiate Church of Our Lady of the Olive Tree (Nossa Senhora da Oliveira). The museum houses old stone carvings from the convent in a 13th-century cloister, as well as rooms filled with gold, ceramics and religious items. There is also a room devoted to the battle of Aljubarrota (see p.16) where the exhibits include the shirt worn by João I during the fray.

> **Signs:**
> *entrada livre*–
> **admission free**
> *é proibido tirar fotografias*–**no cameras allowed**

The other museum in Guimarães worth visiting is the **Martins Sarmento Museum**, named after the 19th-century excavator of the Citânia de Briteiros. The Celto-Iberian artefacts on show here, recovered from Briteiros and other sites, include carved-stone lintels, tools and several fascinating sculptures, such as the enormous pre-Roman Colossus of Pedralva.

In the Penha Hills above the city is the lovely **Monastery of Santa Marinha da Costa**. This old building has been restored to form a luxury pousada (see p.178), which is well worth looking around, even if you are not staying.

Briteiros

Between Guimarães and nearby Braga is the prehistoric site of **Briteiros**, set on a rocky hillside overlooking a series of valleys and forested hills. The entire hillside is covered with the remains of the best-preserved *citânia* (Celtic hill settlement) in Portugal. The walls of hundreds of circular houses can be seen (two have been rebuilt), in addition to roads and drainage channels and a defensive wall. Down the hill is a mysterious structure that has been interpreted both as a burial chamber and as a bath house. The most impressive artefacts from the site can be viewed in the Martins Sarmento Museum in Guimarães.

Braga

Braga (22km/13 miles northwest of Guimarães) has more than 30 churches and is the old religious centre of Portugal, famous for its Holy Week celebrations (see p.133). The exterior of the **Sé** (Cathedral) is fairly plain; originally Romanesque, it has been embellished over the years in a number of styles. Inside are two extravagant golden organs, replete with trumpets, and a painted ceiling flanking the nave near the entrance. The true wealth of the Archbishopric of Braga can be glimpsed in the cathedral's **Museum of Religious Art**, crammed with gold and silver, including the cross that Cabral took on his pioneering voyage to Brazil in 1500.

A young Holy Week celebrant in front of Braga's former Palace of the Archbishop.

The pedestrianized Rua do Souto runs right through the middle of town, passing the square of the former **Palace of the Archbishop**, nowadays a library, and an old medieval keep, before reaching the centre at the Praça da Republica, where you will find the tourist office, housed in a marvellous art deco building.

To pilgrims, Bom Jesus offers baroque grandeur in place of the straight and narrow.

Also worth a look is the nearby **Casa dos Biscainhos**, built during the 17th century, though the decoration is 18th-century. The house reflects the refined lifestyle enjoyed by the nobility, with *azulejo* panels showing falconry, displays of Chinese porcelain, and delightful gardens.

One of the most surprising sights is the pilgrimage church of **Bom Jesus**, situated on a mountain 4km (2 miles) east of Braga. The twin-towered church is constructed in the baroque style. Leading up to it is a grand staircase, lined with chapels, lichen-covered statues, urns and fountains. The devout climb all the way up on their knees; the lazy take the funicular railway and stay in one of the three hotels located at the top.

Two other religious sites of particular interest are the rare Visigothic **Chapel of São Frutuoso**, some 3km (2 miles) northwest of Braga, and the strangely eerie and abandoned **Monastery of Tibães**, another 4km (2.5 miles) out.

☞ Barcelos

A short journey west of Braga will take you to **Barcelos**, home of the country's largest agricultural fair. This is held every Thursday in the massive open square, the Campo da

República. Every kind of animal and every sort of produce from the Minho is on sale, as well as the famous pottery and handicrafts of Barcelos.

Traditional music of the Minho in Viana do Castelo (left); the Gothic pillory of Barcelos (below).

In one corner of the square is the beautiful church of
Nossa Senhor Bom Jesus da Cruz, an octagonal baroque
building. The old part of town continues on down to the
River Cávado. The Palace of the Counts of Barcelos overlooks the river, but was abandoned after the 1755 earthquake. Its shell now houses the various stone artefacts
making up the **Archaeological Museum**.

The Minho Coast

The Minho's **Costa Verde** (Green Coast) is very low-key
compared with the crowded beaches of the Algarve. Beautiful beaches run in a virtually unbroken sweep from Oporto
all the way up to the Spanish border on the River Minho.
Since the people who live here do not depend on tourism for
their livelihood, you are more likely to experience the real
Portugal. It is not unusual, for example, to see oxen pulling
carts piled high with seaweed for fertilizer.

There are a number of resorts close to Oporto (see p.48).
Further up the coast is **Esposende**, a slightly bland resort of
Mediterranean-style hotels. The beaches across the estuary
at Ofir, however, are very pleasant. You'll find that the most
beautiful beaches in this area are attached to small coastal
villages, such as **Mar**.

The only major resort along this coastline is the splendid
city of **Viana do Castelo** (60km/38 miles north of Oporto) –
which has a great deal to offer besides beaches. Viana is
bounded by the estuary of the River Lima to the south and by
the wooded Monte de Santa Luzia to the north. The triangular Praça da República forms the centre of the historic old
town, around which are a series of *palácios*, constructed during Viana's heyday as a *bacalhau* centre (see p.138). Especially interesting is the fine 16th-century Renaissance
Misericórdia (Almshouse).

Rising above Viana is the scenic **Monte de Santa Luzia**. Like Bom Jesus (see p.33), it has a pilgrimage church on the summit and a funicular railway, though no grand staircase. The church itself is not beautiful, but the views from the plaza in front take in the north and south coast, the River Lima and Viana itself. There is also a fine 1930s hotel (see p.178) and an excavated *citânia* (pre-Roman hillfort) faintly reminiscent of Briteiros (see p.31).

Viana's main beach lies to the south, across the estuary at **Praia do Cabedelo**, accessible by ferry or road bridge. Heading north along the coast from Viana there is little sand, but the rocks are popular for fishing. The small, quaint resort town of **Vila Praia de Âncora** is a further 16km (10 miles) up the coast.

The River Lima

Inland from Viana do Castelo, the beautiful flat Lima Valley runs east through a gentle agricultural landscape dotted with

Flower markets abound.

haystacks. The Romans settled this attractive area as soon as they had sorted out their initial confusion between the Lima and the legendary Lethe, the River of Forgetfulness.

Having traversed the river and survived, memory intact, they built a bridge at **Ponte de Lima**, 23km (14 miles) upstream from Viana. This is a pleasant town, named after the Roman bridge (*ponte*) that still spans the Lima. It has wide sandbanks on the southern side of the river where an ancient bi-monthly market is held (they also provide a good place for a swim). The hills on the north side offer scenic walks. Ponte de Lima also has an excellent choice of accommodation in old manor houses – as befits the home of the Turismo de Habitação scheme (see *Accommodation*, p.150).

Ponte de Barca (18km/11 miles further east along the Lima) will also appeal if you like Ponte de Lima. It, too, is home to a fine bridge (though this one is 15th-century), and it hosts a bi-monthly market by the river. The town serves as a good base for some pleasant hill walks, past unspoilt, small Minho villages.

Although not strictly in the Lima Valley, nearby **Arcos de Valdevez**, set in the deep valley of the River Vez, shares many of the same attributes and is well worth a leisurely, relaxing visit.

The Peneda-Gerês National Park

The Lima Valley continues east towards the river's source in Spain, passing through the wild and wonderful **Peneda-Gerês National Park**. Although this is one of the most visited parts of the Minho, it is very easy to hike up into the mountains and find yourself alone with the mountain goats. Fifteen species of wild flower appear only in the park, and a further 26 are very rare outside it. The park boasts mountains, river valleys, megalithic monuments (*antas*), water-

WILD AND BEAUTIFUL PLACES

Portugal boasts much spectacular scenery and natural splendour. The list below highlights some of its greatest features.

Minho: the rugged mountains of the Peneda-Gerês National Park (see p.37) and the gentle beauty of the Lima Valley (see p.37).

The Douro Valley: the River Douro winding its long course through the port-wine vineyards (see p.50).

Trás-os-Montes: the ancient hill villages of the Serra de Montesinho, still the haunt of wolves and boars, and the deep,

The rough beauty of the Serra da Estrêla, the highest mountains in Portugal.

dramatic gorge of the Alto Douro (see p.60).

The Beiras: the river estuary, salt marsh and lagoon at Aveiro (see p.70) and the peaks of Portugal's highest mountains in the Serra da Estrêla National Park (pictured left) (see p.75).

Estremadura and Ribatejo: the seabird colonies of Berlenga Island (see p.86), the flowers and jagged peaks of the Serra da Arrábida (see p.82), and the birds of the Tagus estuary (see p.89).

Lisbon: the tropical greenhouses of the Eduardo VII Park (see p.99).

Alentejo: the River Guadiana flowing down to the Algarve (see p.112) and the rolling hills of the Serra de São Mamede (see p.109).

Algarve: the wooded hills and stark mountains of the Serra de Monchique (see p.123) and the wild, lonely cliffs of the Sagres Peninsula (see p.124).

falls and small mountain hamlets. Numerous tracks criss-cross the area, passing reservoirs that are perfect for a dip after a long day's hike.

The park is divided into two parts: the much-visited Serra do Gerês, and the quieter, wilder Serra da Peneda to the north. **Caldas do Gerês** is the principal tourist base, complete with its own spa. Hiking advice is available from the park information office, and the tourist office can provide details of local accommodation and outdoor activities, such as horse trekking. The nearby Miradouro do Gerês gives a marvellous view over much of the park.

The best approach to the northern Peneda section of the park is from either Monção or Melgaço, on the River Minho. The main point of access for the eastern part of the park is Caldas do Gerês, but there is another fascinating route starting from Chaves (see p.56), in Trás-os-Montes, that crosses a truly remote area before, surprisingly, taking you past the gigantic **Pisões dam**.

The River Minho

The River Minho forms the northern border between the Minho (Portugal) and Galicia (Spain). As a result, its banks are lined by numerous beautiful walled towns and powerful fortresses. The charming town of **Vila Nova de Cerveira**, about 20km (12 miles) northeast from the coastal resort of Vila Praia de Âncora, is typical, with its town walls and a regular ferry service across the river to Spain. Inside the walls of the old fortress is a luxurious pousada.

Further upriver, **Valença do Minho** boasts dramatic and powerful defensive walls (also housing a pousada). Inside is a well-preserved town of winding streets and 17th-century buildings. Its defences face those of Tui, across the river in Spain, which is now connected by a bridge. Hordes of Span-

Excellent fresh produce can be obtained from street vendors all around the country.

ish day-trippers come across to shop, but leave the town in peace by nightfall.

Monção, 16km (10 miles) to the east, has survived many Spanish sieges, often pulling through by means of such ingenious strategies as giving away their last scraps of food to the besieging troops to convince them that they had more than enough. The fortress is not as impressive as some others along the river, but the old town boasts several pleasing churches, including the Romanesque Igreja da Matriz, and the Igreja da Misericórdia, with its wonderful *azulejos*. The town also hosts a lively market on Thursday.

Melgaço, Portugal's most northerly town, sits alone in the northeastern Minho, little visited by tourists, as not much happens here. Its peacefulness however makes it a very relaxing place (market on Friday). It is a good access point into the dramatic northern section of the Peneda-Gerês National Park (see p.37).

OPORTO AND THE DOURO VALLEY

Oporto (from *O Porto*, meaning simply 'The Port') is situated in a dramatic gorge at the mouth of the Douro river, and is Portugal's second city (after Lisbon). Oporto's history is long: it was the site of the town of Portus in the Roman era.

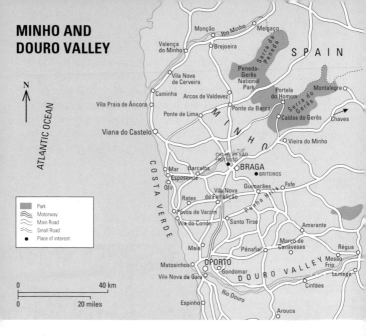

MINHO AND DOURO VALLEY

Together with its twin town of Calus, on the opposite bank, it came to be known as Portucale in the early Middle Ages, and from this came the name of the whole country of Portugal. Despite its importance, Oporto is less self-conscious than Lisbon: its citizens know they live in a nice place and don't feel the need to show off about it, preferring just to get on with their business. Walking is the best way to explore the city, though you'll find there are many hills, down which the jumble of tile-roofed buildings spill to the river.

The river has always been the source of Oporto's wealth. The Douro flows all the way across from the Spanish border, snaking past the terraced vineyards of the Douro Valley.

These vineyards produce several fine wines and, most famously of all, the rich fortified wine known as port – after Oporto. Traditionally the port used to be shipped down the raging torrent in barrels on *barcos rabelos* (flat-bottomed square-sailed boats) to the port lodges (merchants' warehouses) of Vila Nova de Gaia, just opposite Oporto. The river is now dammed and thus made safe for scenic upriver cruises to the *quintas* (agricultural estates) of the Douro, around the town of Régua.

☞ Oporto

The **Praça da Liberdade** marks the centre of the town, though this lies outside the old walls and is home to nothing more interesting than 19th-century bank façades. Not far from here is the tourist office, up Avenida dos Aliados and beside the City Hall, at Rua Clube Fenianos 25. Also near the Praça is the ornate **Estação de São Bento**, far too beautiful to be a mere railway station. The interior is covered with wonderful *azulejo* panels depicting important scenes from the city's history.

For a splendid view over Oporto's confusing jumble of streets, head west out of the Praça, down Rua Clérigos, and climb the tower of the imposing baroque **Clérigos church**. The tower is also a good landmark around which to work your sightseeing.

The **Cathedral** (Sé) is a typical 12th-century Romanesque building, bare and austere – more a fortress than a church. In the 18th century, an attempt was

Oporto's Dom Luís I Bridge (below); Vila Nova de Gaia is a mecca for lovers of port (right).

made to liven it up with some baroque additions to the façade, but this was largely unsuccessful. Inside the cathedral, a beautiful baroque silver altarpiece is worth a look, as is the rose window. Within these granite walls, João I married his English bride, Philippa of Lancaster, in 1387 (the scene is depicted in *azulejos* in São Bento railway station), thus sealing the ancient alliance between Portugal and England – an alliance that has always remained particularly strong in Oporto, on account of the English involvement in the port-wine trade.

As you head away from the cathedral towards the river, the land slopes downward and the streets turn into steep and confusing alleys. This area, the medieval **Barredo**, is one of the most picturesque parts of the city. Delightful little hole-in-the-wall shops line the ancient streets, steep as a ladder, and outside every other house, it seems, hang great racks of multi-coloured laundry. Here, too, you will come across the Renaissance Jesuit church, **Igreja dos Grilos**.

The riverside quay, the **Cais da Ribeira**, is geared towards satisfying hungry diners. Here you'll find innumerable informal restaurants serving many styles of food, though nearly all offering seafood. The impressive **Dom Luís I Bridge** (1886) rears over the colourful houses of the Ribeira and leads across to the south bank, where the port lodges of Vila Nova de Gaia are situated (see p.46). Tour boats tie up here and offer short river tours, beneath the city's scenic bridges, as well as week-long trips up the Douro to Régua (see p.52). Also worth a look is the interesting Centro Regional de Artes Tradicionais (Regional Arts Centre), with its shop.

Many restaurants offer a *Prato do dia* (dish of the day) that often provides a good meal at a fair price.

Just uphill from the river is the **Bolsa** district, named after the elegant 19th-century Stock Exchange (Bolsa) on the Praça do Infante Dom Henrique. Guided tours are available to show you around the opulent interior, including the highlight of the Salão Arabe (Arab Room), where the Moorish style of the Alhambra in Granada is lavishly recreated.

Next door is the city's finest church, the **Igreja de São Francisco**, which was once attached to a monastery. Looking like a conventional Gothic church from the outside, the inside resembles an explosion in a gold factory. Gilded rococo details cover the walls from ground to ceiling – the most

The Arab Room of Oporto's old Stock Exchange is notable for its extravagance.

impressive part being the Tree of Jesse on the northern wall. A small museum opposite the church displays relics of the old monastery.

Also near the Bolsa is the **Casa do Infante**, supposedly the site, if not the actual building, where Henry the Navigator was born (see p.17). Some ship models and documents are on display. The *tripeiros* ('tripe eaters', as people from Oporto are known) are very proud of their association with Henry, especially as Oporto was where the fleet for the 1415 assault on Ceuta was fitted out. For this patriotic venture against the Moors of North Africa, the people of Oporto surrendered the finest cuts of meat in their stores to the navy and lived on tripe instead, thus earning their honourable nickname.

☞ Vila Nova de Gaia

The lower level of the Dom Luís I Bridge leads to the port lodges (warehouses) of **Vila Nova de Gaia**, which are the low buildings on the southern bank, with company names painted in white on the roofs. The upper level of the bridge affords a wonderful view of the city and runs across to the former convent of Nossa Senhora da Serra do Pilar.

Although it is no longer required by law, most port is still stored and aged in the lodges (*armazéns*) of Vila Nova de Gaia. Almost all were founded after the Treaty of Methuen in 1703, under which the English agreed to reduce the tariffs on port-wine imports. Many companies give free tours of their lodges, explaining the production process and offering visitors a free sample. You can choose whether to tour one of the large-scale concerns (such as Sandeman), or the smaller, more intimate lodges of firms such as Calém or Fonseca.

Oporto's Major Museums

It is best to check with the tourist office whether a particular museum is open, as many have been undergoing renovation recently. Generally museums are open from Tuesday to Saturday, though some also open on Sunday.

The **Museum of Ethnography and History** (Museu de Etnografia e História) at Largo de São João Novo (near the Bolsa) is located in an 18th-century mansion and has an eclectic collection of regional art and costume, glass, ceramics and jewellery.

The **Fernando de Castro Museum** (Casa Museu Fernando de Castro) at Rua de Costa Cabral 176 (2km/1 mile northeast of Clérigos) houses a collection of relics from various old monasteries.

The **Guerra Junqueiro Museum** (Casa Museu Guerra Junqueiro), Rua de Dom Hugo (near the cathedral), is the former home of the poet, Guerra Junqueiro, and displays his furniture and collection of art.

The **Modern Art Museum** (Museu Nacional de Arte Moderna), Rua Serralves 977 (about 3km/2 miles west of Clérigos), is housed in a 1930s building, surrounded by a fine park, and was established by the Gulbenkian Foundation to display the work of contemporary Portuguese artists and designers (with frequent exhibition changes).

The **Romantic Museum and Port Institute** (Museu Romântico and Solar do Vinho do Porto), Quinta da Macieir-

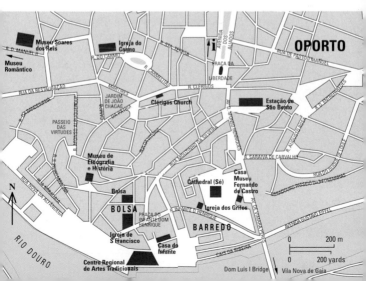

inha, Rua Entre-Quintas 220 (west of Clérigos), displays a collection of 19th-century art and furniture in the last home of the deposed King of Sardinia. Downstairs is the Solar do Vinho do Porto, where you will find hundreds of port vintages waiting to be sampled.

The **Soares dos Reis Museum** (Museu Nacional Soares dos Reis), Palácio dos Carrancas, Rua Dom Manuel II (west of Clérigos), is a wonderful collection of fine art housed in an 18th-century palace. Portuguese artists, from the 15th to the 20th centuries, are well represented, including paintings by Josefa de Óbidos and sculptures by Soares dos Reis. Also on display are goods that once formed the basis of Portuguese trade with the Orient, especially ceramics.

Oporto is one of Portugal's most important cities, second only to Lisbon.

The **Teixeira Lopes Museum** (Museu Lopes), Rua Teixeira Lopes 16/42 (Vila Nova de Gaia), highlights the work of Teixeira Lopes (star student of the sculptor, Soares dos Reis), and his turn-of-the-century artistic circle.

Coastal Excursions

Oporto's nearest beaches lie to the west, where the Douro passes a large sandbar and meets the sea at **Foz do Douro** (Mouth of the Douro). This was a very popular resort in the 19th century, but the water is now heavily polluted. Nevertheless, the beaches and restaurants still make an enjoyable day out, and a scenic old tram (number 18) provides excursions from the resort to the 17th-century Castelo do Queijo (Cheese Castle).

There is another beach at **Matosinhos** (near the airport), though the water here also is polluted and overlooked by a giant industrial complex.

Further to the north, the beach resorts of the Minho's Costa Verde (see p.35) are at least clean, even if they are none too warm. The nearest to Oporto is the twin resort area of Vila do Conde/Póvoa de Varzim, 27km (16 miles) to the north. **Vila do Conde** is the more pleasant and less developed of the two. It sits where the River Ave meets the sea, and owes its growth to fishing and ship building. The enormous Convento de Santa Clara looks over the old town, though it is not open to the public. What is worth a visit, however, is the 16th-century **Igreja Matriz**, with its mix of Gothic and Manueline details. The Friday market is fun, but the main reason why people come here is the beach, which stretches south of the town.

Póvoa do Varzim is a short walk north from Vila do Conde, but is a much livelier and more built-up resort, with a casino. An interesting diversion inland from here is to **Rates**, where you can add a dash of culture to the days spent on the beach by looking around the marvellous Romanesque church.

Espinho, 20km (12 miles) south along the coast, is a large, if unlovely, resort where the water is clean. There are many hotels amongst the grid of streets, and consequently many tourists, but the beach is large enough to accommodate everybody. Further south, towards Aveiro (see p.70), there is rather less development and fewer people.

The Lower Douro Valley

Douro Valley cruises run from the Ribeira, in Oporto, up to Régua and Pinhão, some lasting only a day and others a whole week. Other cruises run between Pinhão all the way to Barca d'Alva, near the border with Spain. Alternatively, you can travel up or down the length of the Douro Valley by train

Port Wine

Port in English, Vinho de Porto in Portuguese, the fortified wine of the Douro Valley is justly famous throughout the world. It first became popular outside the region during the Middle Ages. The English, cut off from French sources of wine because of war, grew especially fond of port. English merchants later became heavily involved in the trade, particularly after the 1703 Methuen Treaty (see p.22), and founded many 'factories', such as Croft, Sandeman and Cockburn.

The Marquês de Pombal regulated the industry in the 18th century by creating the world's first demarcated wine-growing region and introducing rules to prevent adulteration of the port.

Port wine was once like any other wine. The fortified wine of today only developed when grape brandy was added to stabilize the wine during its long journey overseas. It was discovered that this had the effect of halting the fermentation and leaving a fresh sweet flavour that deepened as the wine aged.

A vintage is declared when growers reach a consensus that there has been an outstanding year. Ruby port is a red and fruity variety, while tawny is a lighter, more golden colour. One kind not well known outside Portugal is white port (porto branco), made with white grapes and served as a pre-meal drink – other varieties are consumed at the end of the meal.

– a spectacular ride. For further information contact the tourist office in Oporto.

Heading upriver from the sandbank at its mouth, the Douro runs between Oporto and the port lodges of Vila Nova de Gaia, passing beneath a series of impressive bridges and on towards port-wine territory. The railway line from Oporto skips the first 60km (37 miles) of the river, but this is the least interesting stretch. It eventually joins the river near **Ribadouro**, proceeding along the northern bank, past small towns and fields where the haystacks, set on cross-shaped supports, look from a distance like scarecrows.

Green wooded hills reach down to the river, which bends and twists, widens and narrows. The river is nowadays dammed, so the water is very still and reflects the terraced hills. The freezing winters and hot summers make for an unusual micro-climate that fosters the area's famous grapes.

The devout scale the steps of Lamego's church on their knees, unheedful of its splendour.

These steep vineyards (below) yield fine grapes – a cause for celebration (right), no less.

During the harvest (*vindima*) in late September and early October, the land comes alive as whole communities gather together for the picking of the grapes. Some of the grapes are crushed by foot, to the accompaniment of guitar music, though most are now crushed by mechanical means.

The port trade was responsible for the growth of **Régua** (full name Peso da Régua), approximately 70km (43 miles) east of Oporto. This was once the main port for shipping the partly made wine downriver in flat-bottomed *rabelo* boats to Vila Nova de Gaia. The railways took over for transport from Pinhão (at the confluence of the Douro and Pinhão rivers), and now the wine goes mostly by road.

Even so, the headquarters of the winegrowers, the Casa do Douro, has remained in Régua, as have a number of port cellars. Sandeman has a large modern winery just across the

river, and Cockburns is up the hill overlooking Régua. One of the best ways to get an insight into the world of port is to stay at one of the numerous *quintas* (country mansions) in the area (see *Accommodation*, p.150), which virtually all produce their own port.

The town of **Mesão Frio**, 12km (7 miles) west of Régua, is another great place to relax, high above the Douro. Here you'll find many beautiful *solares* (manor houses), some of which offer accommodation.

The prettiest town in the area is the affluent centre of **Lamego**, south of the Douro, 13km (8 miles) from Régua. Although officially part of the Beiras, its soul is really of the Douro. As well as growing grapes for port, Lamego also produces a fine champagne-like wine called Raposeira. Lamego was once a pilgrimage centre, hence the elaborate baroque church of Nossa Senhora dos Remédios and the stunning stone staircase leading up to it. The design of the staircase was inspired by that of Bom Jesus (see p.33), and is lined with statues, *azulejos*, fountains and chapels. Some pilgrims climb the 600-plus steps on their knees, especially during the great pilgrimage on 8 September.

Lamego also has a scenic 13th-century castle and a 16th-century cathedral with a 12th-century tower. The Museu de Lamego, in the old bishop's palace, houses a fine collection of Flemish tapestries and religious statues, as well as five paintings by Grão Vasco, of the Viseu school (see p.73).

Amarante, on the Tâmega (a tributary of the Douro), makes a handy stop if you are driving along the road from Oporto towards Mesã Frio and Régua. The church of the former monastery of São Gonçalo is well worth a visit, especially if you are looking for love: it hosts a pilgrimage in June for women seeking husbands.

TRÁS-OS-MONTES

Trás-os-Montes is a unique area of Europe. This land 'Beyond the Mountains' is Portugal's poorest and most remote region, made up of deep river valleys separated by rocky hilltops and dense forests. The region retains a medieval air, and old ideas survived here long after the rest of Europe moved on. Development funds from the European Union and the influence of returning migrants have introduced an element of the modern, but if you drive out into the countryside (a car is strongly recommended) you will see that a much older peasant way of life has remained for the average shepherd and his flock.

The isolation of the mountains made life almost unbearable for the troops that used to be stationed in the numerous fortresses poised against the Spanish frontier. This same isolation attracted Jews escaping from the Inquisition, and to this day a classic dish of the area is sausage, made with turkey instead of pork.

The northern part (known as Terra Fria, the 'Cold Land') has very harsh winters, while Terra Quente ('Hot Land') is more temperate and includes large vineyards in the Upper Douro Valley. The region also has numerous orchards, and the almond blossom in spring is one of the most sublime sights in Portugal.

Vila Real and the Southwest

Vila Real is the largest town in the region, with a population of 30,000. Mostly modern and industrial, it sits on the edge of the impressive deep gorge of the River Corgo, a tributary of the Douro. A scenic way of reaching Vila Real is by means of the narrow-gauge train from Peso da Régua (see p.52). Vila Real itself may not be fascinating, but there are many interesting sights nearby, and the Alvão and Marão mountain ranges rise abruptly just outside town, making this a good base for hiking.

At the centre of the town is the broad Avenida Carvalho Araújo. Here you will find the cathedral, and the tourist office inside an old mansion. If you continue south, you will pass the 14th-century Capela de São Bras and be rewarded by a fine view of the gorge.

The top sight in the area is the magnificent 18th-century baroque mansion known as the **Solar de Mateus**, about 3km (2 miles) from Vila Real. Its Italianate façade may be familiar, as it appears on bottles of Mateus Rosé (although there is no connection). You can take a guided tour of the interior, but the exterior and gardens are the most evocative features.

Nearby is the small Roman site of **Panóias**, where the only remains are some carved stones that once served as sacrificial altars. Also close by is the village of **Sabrosa**, famous for producing that greatest of globetrotters, Fernão de Magalhães (Ferdinand Magellan), as well as a very good wine.

For a taste of the countryside, visit the small **Parque Natural de Alvão**, just northwest of Vila Real. In winter the hills are covered in snow, but during summer the fields abound with wildflowers and the streams are fed by spectacular waterfalls. The park headquarters, in Vila Real, can give you detailed information.

Chaves and the Northwest

Once past Vila Real, Trás-os-Montes becomes noticeably wilder. The road to Chaves follows a scenic route along the valley of the Corgo. **Vidago** is an elegant 19th-century spa town, 17km (11 miles) before Chaves, boasting the Edwar-

The white stucco and carefully carved stonework
of the Solar de Mateus, near Vila Real.

dian Palace Hotel, gardens and a nine-hole golf course. The spa is only open in summer.

Chaves, a mere 12km (7 miles) from Spain, is a quiet place, when it isn't being attacked by the Spanish. The last military attack took place in 1912, but waves of Spanish shoppers still descend on the town every weekend in search of bargain prices. The town's strategic role as a border crossing is reflected in its name (Chaves means 'Keys') and by its two 17th-century fortresses. There is also a 14th-century keep, which today houses a Military Museum.

> **Surprisingly, French, not Spanish, is the second language most spoken in Portugal.**

Chaves was an important Roman spa town, known as Aquae Flaviae, and its hot springs (good for rheumatism and gout) remain open in summer. The Romans also built a bridge over the River Tâmega, which is still in use and retains its ancient milestone. You can learn more about the Roman past in the Regional Museum on the Praça Camões. Nearby you will find several interesting medieval squares and two fine churches.

Long before the Romans arrived, the region's prehistoric inhabitants left a series of carvings on a massive granite boulder at **Outeiro Machado**, 3km (2 miles) outside Chaves. The carved symbols are believed to have been associated with rituals involving sacrifice – easy to believe in this otherworldly setting.

From Chaves, there is easy access into Spain, and across to the Peneda-Gerês National Park (see p.37) in the Minho. On the way to the Minho, you pass through the marvellous **Serra do Barroso**, approximately 25km (15 miles) west of Chaves. This is an ideal area to explore if you want to get a feel for the Transmontane countryside. **Montalegre**, the largest town in the region, is a rather lonely place dominated by a sombre 14th-century castle; there are also many small villages worth a visit, such as **Vilarinho Sêco**, or the Iron-Age fort at **Carvalhelos**.

Bragança and the Northeast

The route from Chaves to Bragança is particularly attractive, with the road winding over mountain passes, through pine forests and past the spines of bare, rocky hillsides. The new and partially completed houses of returned emigrants stand out from the simpler houses strung alongside fields still worked by donkey plough.

Like most frontier towns in Trás-os-Montes, **Bragança** is a remote outpost, dominated by its citadel and by the bleak surrounding hills. It was here that Catherine of Bragança, the wife of the English king, Charles II, was born. She took with her to England the custom of drinking afternoon tea, and control of Bombay, thus beginning England's interest in India. Catherine's family served as rulers of Portugal between 1640 and 1910, but they preferred their estate at Vila Viçosa in the Alentejo (see p.109) to this lonely vastness.

Bragança's great **Citadel** (Citadella) commands the entire area and is really a small city in its own right. Within its ramparts a whole community goes about its life, living in the small, medieval houses, each with its own garden. The central keep sits on the highest ground and houses a fascinating **Military Museum**, tracing the course of Portuguese military concerns from prehistoric times right through to the colonial wars of the 1970s. Just down from the keep is Portugal's most curious *pelourinho*. Pillories like this were often placed at the centre of Portuguese towns for the punishment of miscreants. This one stands on top of a granite boar, carved in prehistoric times.

The commanding walls of the Citadel at Bragança enclose an entire village.

Also in the citadel is the whitewashed **Igreja de Santa Maria**, with its wavy entrance columns and a lovely painted ceiling. Next door stands a rare example of a 12th-century **Meeting House** (Domus Municipalis). It has five sides, and the upper floor, decorated with Romanesque arches under a timber roof, was used for assemblies, while the lower floor served as a water cistern.

In the lower town, the unusual **Museu Regional Abade de Baçal** is worth a visit, as it is located in the former Bishop's Palace and has an eclectic mix of local archaeological finds, clerical items, regional paintings and costumes. Train spotters will delight in the little **Transport Museum** in the old railway station, where displays include old steam trains and royal carriages.

Two churches worth a look are the Renaissance **Igreja de São Bento**, with its beautiful *trompe l'oeil* ceiling, and the

Igreja de São Vicente, where Pedro I claimed to have married Inês de Castro (see p.87).

☞ The barren and wild **Parque Natural de Montesinho** lies between Bragança and Spain, and is home to a number of small, isolated villages which have striven to keep up their traditions of communal ownership and pre-Christian ritual. They share this landscape with wolves and boars. For details of campsites, visit the park office in Bragança. The village of **Rio Onor**, 24km (15 miles) to the northeast, straddles the border, and here the locals speak a mixed dialect.

> On winding mountain roads it's compulsory to sound your horn.

To the east, towards Miranda do Douro, the land becomes gentler and the hills smaller and rounder. **Outiero**, 32km (20 miles) east of Bragança, looks like many villages must have done once, with the huge church of Santo Cristo dominating the small, unassuming houses grouped around it.

☞ Miranda do Douro

On the very eastern limits of Trás-os-Montes, **Miranda do Douro** stands poised at the edge of the great gorge of the Alto Douro (Upper Douro). Mists descend over the modern dam that has flooded the gorge to a depth of 60m (196 feet). Halfway across the dam, Spain begins.

Miranda itself is a 'city' of 2,000 inhabitants, whose low whitewashed houses and cobbled streets are enclosed by walls to keep the Spanish out. This they singularly failed to do in 1762, when a force of French and Spanish troops blew up the castle, leaving it a fairly uninspiring ruin.

The event led Miranda to lose its bishop, who decamped to the safety of Bragança. The dark and austere 16th-century **cathedral** remains. Its nave is short, with an open-plan de-

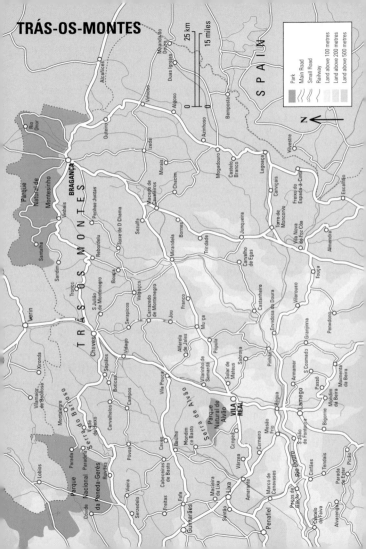

TRÁS-OS-MONTES

25 km
15 miles

Park
Main Road
Small Road
Railway
Land above 100 metres
Land above 200 metres
Land above 500 metres

N

SPAIN

Mofandão Duas Igrejas
Alcañices
Duas Igrejas
Vimioso
Algoso
Azinhoso
Bemposta
Outeiro
Rio Onor
Izeda
Mofadouro
Castelo Branco
Lagoaça
Vilvestre
Parque Natural de Montesinho
Santalha
Vinhais
BRAGANÇA
Peñas Juntas
Torre de D Chama
Rebordelo
Sardinha
S Julião de Montenegro
Bouça
Ferradelo
Verin
Xironda
Serapicos
Carrazedo de Montenegro
Vilar de Peixes
Chaves
Boticas
Sapiãos
Vidago
Jou
Franco
Mirandela
Romeu
Trindade
Carvalho de Egas
Junqueira
Torre de Moncorvo
Vila Nova de Foz Côa
Escalhão
Almendra
Foûça
Vilarouco
Castanheiro
Envedosa do Douro
Penedono
Murças
Alfarela de Jales
Populo
Sabrosa
Pinhão
Granjinha
S Cosmado
Armamar
Momenta da Beira
Vilamaior de Boalhosa
Montalegre
Paradela
Serra do Barroso
Parada
Lobios
Côrte
Parque Nacional da Peneda-Gerês
Boticas
Carvalhelos
Campos
Vila Pouca
Vilarinho de Samardã
Solar de Mateus
VILA REAL
Parque Natural de Alvão
Serra de Alvão
Cerva
Mondim de Basto
Povoa
Cabeceiras de Basto
Ribas
Lixa
Celorico de Basto
Fridão
Vieira
Fafe
Serzedelo
GUIMARÃES
Amarante
Penafiel
Marco de Canaveses
Paços de Ferreira
Castelo de Paiva
Alvarenga
Escariz
Freixo do Espada à Cinta
Lamego
Bigorne
S João de Fontoura
Régua
Passô
Mondim da Beira
Bagúste
Sintrão
Maciera da Lixa
Fratéis
S João de Fontoura
Rio Douro
Cinfães
Tendais
Parada do Sil
Picão
Cernaneiro
Várzea

sign. In the right-hand transept is a statue of a boy, known as the Menino Jesus da Cartolina. Sporting hand-tailored clothes, the little figure commemorates a 16th-century boy-hero who saved the city from the Spanish. Locals believed he was Jesus come down in disguise.

On Largo Dom João III, at the centre of the town, is the excellent **Terra de Miranda Museum**, displaying a selection of traditional Mirandês clothing and wares. Miranda has its own culture and a distinctive dialect, Mirandês, that freely combines Latin, Portuguese, Spanish and even some Hebrew. The town is also renowned for its unique sword dancers, called the *pauliteiros*.

The **gorge** itself is about 2km (1 mile) away, down a twisting road. The rocky hillsides on both sides of the dam are home to some 80 species of bird, as well as flocks of hardy sheep. You can stroll across the dam to Spain, and even stay or eat in the building that once housed the engineers who built the dam, since this is now a pousada (see p.180) with a wonderful view. Cruise boats on the dammed side of the gorge enable you to explore further upriver. On the other side of the dam, the river snakes its way through port-wine country down to Oporto.

Central and Southeastern Trás-os-Montes

Mirandela is a pleasant town that sits at the hub of the region's road system, 54km (33 miles) southeast of Chaves, 64km (40 miles) southwest of Bragança and 70km (43 miles) northeast of Vila Real. The town lies among orchards in the valley of the Tua river. The bridge over the river is a 15th-century construction, built on a Roman base, and measures an impressive 200m (660 feet). The old town contains cobbled streets and is dominated by the 17th-century town hall, home of the Távora family until the Marquês de Pombal had them all executed on a trumped-up charge of treason. The Modern Art Gallery is worth a visit.

Halfway between Vila Real and Mirandela is the small town of **Murça**, most famous for its prehistoric carved stone pig (see below), which lives on a platform in the main square.

Further south and east, in the Upper Douro region, the climate is noticeably warmer. The eccentrically named town of **Freixo do Espada-à-Cinta** ('Ash Tree of the Belted Sword') is where, according to legend, the 13th-century Dom Dinis hung his sword. He also built the town's seven-sided tower. Today it is the almond, rather than the ash, that attracts visitors; the spring blossoms in the local orchards are truly beautiful. The impressive Igreja de Matriz (the parish church) was

---

Portugal's Pigs

Pork has always been a favourite food in Portugal, served in dishes such as pork with clams (porco à Alentejana), suckling pig (leitão), and various smoked hams and sausages. Moorish distaste for pork did not outlast their departure, though the Jews did use turkey to replace pork in their alheira sausages.

This love of the pig seems to be very old, especially in Trás-os-Montes, where prehistoric boars (berrões), carved out of granite, abound. Most are fairly crude and measure about 1.5m (5 feet) in length. Some 200 have been found, but their purpose and date is disputed. Some say they played a part in Celtic fertility rites, while others claim they date from the earlier Iberian period, or the later Roman era. They may have been presented to the gods as an offering to ensure the health of the donor's animals. Similar stone pigs are found in central Spain. The most famous example is the Porco de Murça (see above), and the strangest is the pillory pig of Bragança (see p.58).

---

rebuilt in 1520 in the Manueline style and has a magnificent painting attributed to Grão Vasco (see p.73).

THE BEIRAS

The three ancient provinces known as the Beiras together make up the broad swathe of land lying between the Tagus and Douro rivers. The name Beiras means 'edge' or 'rim', hinting at the position these provinces have long occupied at the boundary between the different traditions of northern and southern Portugal. Each of the three provinces retains its own distinctive character, and so offers different delights to the visitor.

The lovely university city of Coimbra dominates the **Beira Litoral** (Coastal Beira). The neighbouring coastline forms part of the Costa de Prata (Silver Coast) and has largely escaped development, though it does have resorts at Figueira da Foz and Aveiro.

Coimbra is home to a large number of dedicated and hard-working artists.

Inland is the spectacular terrain of the **Beira Alta** (Upper Beira). At this point the small granite hills begin to develop into great mountains, clothed in pine trees and supporting a pastoral way of life. The population is small and the number of tourists few, despite the strange beauty of the landscape, with its giant boulders and flowery meadows. The Serra da Estrêla is the backbone of the area and offers a host of wonderful val-

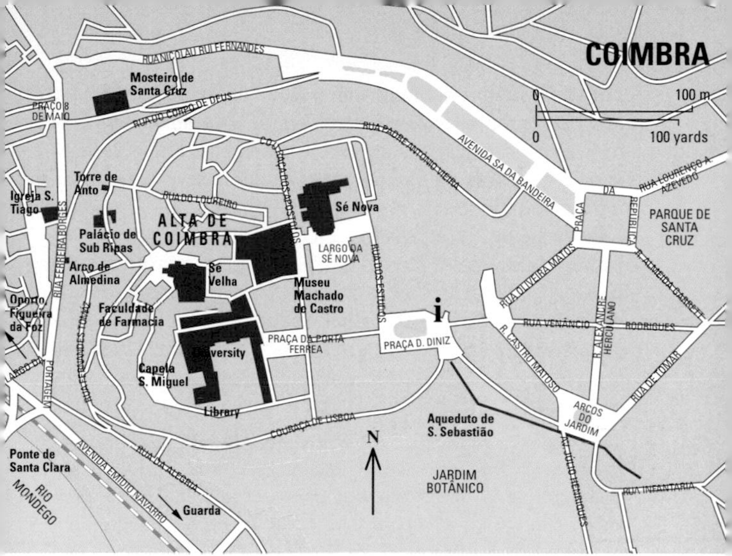

COIMBRA
0
100 m
0
100 yards
RUA NICOLAU RUI FERNANDES
Mosteiro de Santa Cruz
RUA DO CORPO DE DEUS
RUA PADRE ANTÓNIO VIEIRA
AVENIDA SÁ DA BANDEIRA
PRAÇA DA REPÚBLICA
PARQUE DE SANTA CRUZ
Torre de Anto
RUA DO LOUREIRO
Igreja S. Tiago
ALTA DE COIMBRA
Sé Nova
Palácio de Sub Ripas
LARGO DA SÉ NOVA
Arco de Almedina
Sé Velha
Museu Machado de Castro
RUA DOS ESTUDOS
RUA OLIVEIRA MATOS
R. ALMEIDA GARRETT
Oporto, Figueira da Foz
Faculdade de Farmacia
RUA FERREIRA BORGES
RUA VENÂNCIO RODRIGUES
R. ALEXANDRE HERCULANO
R. CASTRO MATOSO
PRAÇA DA PORTA FERREA
PRAÇA D. DINIZ
University
Capela S. Miguel
Library
RUA DE TOMAR
ARCOS DO JARDIM
Aqueduto de S. Sebastião
COUÇARIA DE LISBOA
N
Ponte de Santa Clara
RIO MONDEGO
AVENIDA EMÍDIO NAVARRO
RUA DA ALEGRIA
Guarda
JARDIM BOTÂNICO
AV. JÚLIO HENRIQUES
RUA INFANTARIA

leys and waterfalls for hikers to explore, fortified by the area's fabulous cheese.

Further south, the mountains give way to the agricultural plains of the **Beira Baixa** (Lower Beira), which lacks the monuments and mountains of its neighbours, but still keeps an unspoilt way of life, well worth discovering.

Coimbra and Around

The marvellous university city of **Coimbra** has been at the centre of Portuguese intellectual life since 1290, and even served as the capital during the 12th and 13th centuries. Today it is a lively city, full of young people, that makes few concessions to the tourist, and is better off for it. The famous **University** sits on top of a hill in the old town, overlooking the River Mondego (the tourist office is beside the river, at

Largo da Portagem). Small streets wind up to the University, hiding several *repúblicas* (halls of residence similar to fraternities and sororities) and numerous small bars that reverberate to the strains of Coimbra's own distinctive version of *fado* (see p.131).

The principal courtyard of the University is surrounded by historic buildings on three sides, leaving the fourth open to the river. To the left is the wonderful baroque **Library**, built with João V's fantastic Brazilian wealth in 1720 (he was also responsible for the great Mafra Library, see p.85). Three ex-

---

The Flying Monk

An eccentric product of the Portuguese Age of Enlightenment was the monk and inventor, Padre Bartolomeu Lourenço de Gusmão. He was born in Brazil in 1685. On moving to Portugal he published a treatise on air navigation – immediately dismissed as the work of a madman. In 1709, to answer his critics he built three hot-air balloons and flew them from the Casa da Índia, in Lisbon's Castelo São Jorge, in front of an astonished audience. This earned him the nickname 'O Voador' (The Flying Man) and his invention was dubbed 'A Passarola' (The Big Bird), but without financial backing it went no further.

Gusmão then undertook a voyage of scientific discovery around Europe – inventing, among other things, lenses to cook meat using the heat of the sun. On returning to Portugal, he finished a degree in Canon Law at Coimbra University.

Although many of his inventions were very useful, such as a device for pumping water from ships, his increasingly esoteric ideas bred suspicion amongst the officers of the Inquisition, who accused him of sorcery and of conversion to Judaism. He fled to Spain and died, a haunted man, in Toledo in 1724. A fictionalized account of his life exists in José Saramago's novel *Blimunda and Baltasar* (see p.84).

quisitely gilded and painted chambers are home to a wealth of books, written in many languages and on many subjects. On the same side of the courtyard is a **Museum of Sacred Art** and a **chapel** with fine *azulejos* and a massive baroque organ. Directly ahead is the highly ornate ceremonial hall, the **Sala dos Capelos**, the centre of university life since degrees are given out here.

The nearby **Machado de Castro Museum**, located in the former archbishop's palace, has an excellent collection of medieval sculpture and religious paintings. Among the museum's complex of historic buildings is a Moorish tower and Roman crypt which must be explored.

On either side of the museum are Coimbra's two cathedrals, the classical/baroque **Sé Nova** (New Cathedral) and the more interesting **Sé Velha** (Old Cathedral). The latter's remarkably squat Romanesque bulk is reminiscent of the early crusading cathedrals of Lisbon and Oporto. Renaissance detail has been added around the portals, but the

Through the ages, Coimbra University has honed many of the country's great minds.

interior remains fairly stark. A chapel to the right contains a collection of impressive life-size stone carvings of Jesus, Mary and the Twelve Disciples. Be sure not to miss the peaceful Romanesque cloister.

Coimbra also has several interesting religious houses, in particular the **Monastery of Santa Cruz**, renowned for its Manueline detail, the restored **Convento de Santa Clara-a-Velha**, where the lifeless Inês de Castro was crowned (see p.87), and the newer **Convento de Santa Clara-a-Nova**, where the silver tomb of Isabel, the sainted queen of Dom Dinis, is located.

The two Santa Clara convents lie on the south side of the river, as do two splendid places to relax, the **Jardim Botâni-co**, with its plants collected from all over Portugal's farflung

empire, and the children's theme park, **Portugal dos Pequinos**, where many of the country's greatest and most typical buildings are reproduced in miniature.

Portugal's finest Roman remains are to be found 17km (10 miles) south of Coimbra, at **Conimbriga**, close by the pottery town of Condeixa-a-Nova. The extensive site has not yet been fully excavated, but a variety of buildings, with colourful mosaics, fountains, and a heating system, can be seen. In the later stages of the site's history a large wall

A day for attending mass and finding happiness – Sunday and and one of its exponents.

was hurriedly built, passing right through a number of houses, to keep out marauding barbarians, but evidently this was unsuccessful. A large museum displays finds from the area.

Along the Mondego, 28km (17 miles) west of Coimbra, is the sturdy and imposing castle at **Montemor-o-Velho** (home town of the wanderer Fernão Mendes Pinto, see p.19), affording great views. Here, too, is the fine Manueline church of Santa Maria de Alcáçova.

One of the country's most ancient forests is a short 25km (15 miles) north of Coimbra, at **Buçaco**, making for a wonderful daytrip. The forest is home to more than 700 types of tree, and was once the preserve of monks, women not being allowed to enter. Footpaths meander all over the peaceful forest, and if you need a drink or meal after all that walking, you can visit the fantastic Palace Hotel (see p.181). For further relaxation, try the nearby spa town of **Luso**, with its elegant 19th-century buildings, casino and, of course, the spa itself.

Another scenic daytrip from Coimbra is to the villages and woods of the **Serra da Lousã**, 25km (15 miles) to the southeast. Lousã, the main town, has an ancient castle and several fine 18th-century houses; many of the smaller villages around here are now atmospheric ghost towns.

The Coast

The prettiest stretch of coast in the south of the Beira Littoral is near the ancient pine forest of the **Pinhal de Leiria**, where superb beaches can be found at **São Pedro de Moel** (21km/13 miles north of Nazaré).

Lively **Figueira da Foz**, 42km (26 miles) to the west of Coimbra at the mouth of the Mondego, has developed from a fishing village into a fun resort. The town beach is large, while separate smaller beaches cater for surfers and families. Accommodation is adequate, and you'll always find something to do, be it gambling in the casino, admiring the archaeological collections in the Dr Santos Rocha Museum, attending the bullfights or sampling the enormous variety of seafood on offer.

Praia de Mira (35km/22 miles north of Figueira and 6km/4 miles west of the inland town of Mira) is located by a small lagoon. It is characterized by its wooden stilt-houses, and though it lacks the lively nightlife or extensive accommodation of Figueira (camping is available), it does have unspoilt and uncrowded beaches and dunes.

Other than Figueira, the main resort along this stretch of coast is historic **Aveiro**, 52km (32 miles) to the south of Oporto and 29km (18 miles) north of Mira. Aveiro is unique in the way of life that has grown around its lagoon (Ria). It was an important port until 1575, when a sandbar formed across the River Vouga, cutting the port off from the sea and creating a vast lagoon. Ships were unable to enter the stranded port until a canal was cut in 1808. The pleasant town has various Dutch-style canals and bridges. The Aveiro Museum, in the old Convent of Jesus, displays much religious art, though its massive 18th-century Chapel of Princesa Santa Joana is the most interesting sight.

Aveiro's economic life depends largely on the sea. Apart from fishing, the colourful high-prowed *moliceiro* boats are used to collect huge piles of seaweed for use as fertilizer. The extensive salt pans are also exploited. The tourist office on Rua João Mendonça can arrange boat trips to explore this wonderful area and see the rich variety of birdlife.

Aveiro's beaches are out of the town, the nearest being **Praia da Barra** at the mouth of the Vouga. There are many other beaches around, both to the south and to the north towards Espinho (see p.49) and Oporto. **São Jacinto** is a small resort with an excellent bird sanctuary, which offers tours.

Batalha and Fátima

Rising right next to the main Lisbon highway is the confusing mass of flying buttresses and spires that make up the monastery at **Batalha** (literally 'Battle'). This honey-coloured church was built to celebrate João I's important victory over the Castilians at neighbouring Aljubarrota, in 1385. The massive Gothic façade is decorated with dozens of religious statues. Just inside the main door is the Capela do Fundador ('Founder's Chapel') where João and his English queen, Philippa of Lancaster, lie in effigy holding hands.

The nave itself has a high ceiling and is fairly stark. At the east end, however, are the roofless Capelas Inperfeitas (Unfinished Chapels), started by Dom Duarte, but subsequently transformed by the Manueline architect, Mateus Fernandes, into a unique example of unrestrained architecture, with the giant portal covered with all manner of stone detail. The Claustro Real (Royal Cloister) was itself transformed from Gothic to Manueline, with added stone ornamentation and filigree, in the early 16th century. The chapterhouse, off to the side, was an extraordinary engineering feat of the time because of the sheer size of the unsupported ceiling. Now it houses the **Tomb of the Unknown Soldier**. The town of Batalha is dwarfed by the

The striking monastery at Batalha.

Portugal's premier pilgrimage site, Fátima.

monastery and was only built to serve its builders and monks, just as it now serves its many visitors.

Fátima, 18km (11 miles) southeast of Batalha, has become the main Catholic pilgrimage centre in Portugal. It was here that three young shepherds saw a vision of the Virgin Mary on 13 May 1917. The Virgin reappeared on the 13th of every month until 13 October, when thousands witnessed fireballs raining down from the sun. A large neoclassical basilica has been built on the site of the apparition, surrounded by a huge square. Popular pilgrimages are held monthly on the 13th of every month from May to October. Religion is very much the attraction here, there being little else except souvenir shops and a waxworks museum depicting the story of the apparitions.

Between Batalha and Fátima lies the **Parque Natural das Serra de Aire**, with its numerous underground caves. The biggest is at **Mira de Aire** where you can go on a tour through the stalagmites and stalactites and to a deep underground lake. Other less commercial caves are nearby.

A good base for visiting the many sights in the area is the friendly but busy town of **Leiria**, 11km (7 miles) north of Batalha. There is a wonderful view from its historic castle, and the little alleyways of the former Jewish Quarter survive, now home to small cafés and bars.

Beira Alta

Heading away from Coimbra towards Viseu (87km/54 miles northeast), the land becomes much more rural. Small terraced farms, with stone houses, donkeys and grape vines, sit amongst the forested hills. This is the Dão wine region, whose oaky red wines are named after the River Dão, a tributary of the Mondego. Just west of the Dão is the scenic Serra do Caramulo, where invigorating walks can be taken from the village of **Caramulo** (surprisingly home to a car museum, and an art museum with paintings by Picasso and Dalí) through thick vegetation to the peak of Caramulinho (1,075m/3,527ft).

Viseu is a friendly and dignified town with a long history, supposedly home to Viriathus, the Lusitanian hero who organized the opposition to the Roman invasion of 147 BC. The scenic old town is centred around the Praça da Sé, with its central pillory, and historic buildings arranged all around. The bulky twin-towered cathedral was originally Romanesque, but was redesigned in the 17th century. The classical cloister, where you find the art collection, has Ionic columns on the first level and Doric on the second. The other church on the square, the bright white Igreja Misericórdia, has a better (baroque) façade but a less interesting interior.

Probably the finest sight in Viseu, and one of Portugal's most important art museums, is the **Grão Vasco Museum**, also located on the Praça da Sé – in the former archbishop's palace. Vasco Fernandes (the Grão means 'Great') founded the city's

Colourful goods on display in the tiny medieval shopping streets of Viseu.

school of painting in the 16th century, and his works are well represented here, as are those of the various Flemish artists who influenced the Viseu School, and those of Vasco's great Portuguese rival, Gaspar Vaz.

The Planalto

Towards the northeast of the Beira Alta is the barren plateau of the **Planalto** ('High Plain'), a wild, cold and sparsely populated region, but important enough to have been fought over by Portugal and Spain. The plateau's isolation attracted many Jews fleeing the Inquisition. The medieval walled town of **Trancoso** (43km/26 miles to the north of Guarda) records this heritage in the stone carvings above the doorways of Jewish houses, particularly that of the Rabbi. Powerful castle walls enclose a strong keep built by the ever-busy Dom Dinis to strengthen the border against Spain.

Almeida (65km/40 miles east) also boasts strong fortifications, made necessary because of its position right next to the Spanish border. The town is encapsulated within star-shaped Vaubanesque fortifications, reminiscent of those at Elvas in the Alentejo (see p.109). It featured prominently in sieges and countersieges during the Peninsular War, fought against the army of Napoleon, but fortunately it survived to house a pousada.

Guarda and the Serra da Estrêla

Guarda (69km/43 miles east of Viseu) is the highest city in the country (1,040m/3,412ft) and so is often cold and windy. Its reputation is summed up in the four F words: *fria, farta, forte e feia* ('cold, rich, strong and ugly'). At least two of these epithets is deserved. The cathedral is dark and menacing, a mixture of Gothic and Manueline. Some of the Old Town's cobbled streets have survived, as have three gates, the most impressive being the Torre dos Ferreiros ('Tower of the Blacksmiths'). The main reason for coming to Guarda, however, is for access to the nearby mountains.

The **Serra da Estrêla**, just southwest of Guarda, offers Portugal's highest mountains, at 1,991m (6,532ft), and some fantastic scenery for hiking through the Natural Park (Parque Natural). The best base is **Penhas da Saúde**, which also offers Portugal's only ski resort. **Linhares** boasts a scenic castle and a stretch of Roman road, as well as the beauty of granite peaks and high, peaceful mountain meadows, grazed by sheep whose milk is used to make the area's excellent Serra cheese. For further details of hiking routes, ask at the tourist office in Guarda or Covilhã, or at the park information offices in Gouveia, Manteigas or Seia.

Going south from Guarda, a pleasant place to stop after some 20km (12 miles) on the road is **Belmonte**, with its carefully restored 13th-century castle and Jewish Quarter, home to this day to a Jewish community (see p.21).

Covilhã, a further 20km (12 miles) south, has become a base for exploring the Serra because of its location close to the highest peaks and the ski fields. This area produced several explorers: from Covilhã came Pêro de Covilhã, who explored India and Ethiopia in the late 15th century, and from Belmonte came Pedro Álvares Cabral, who laid claim to Brazil in 1500.

Beira Baixa

Contrasting with the mountains to the north is the Lower Beira (Beira Baixa), where – for the most part – agricultural plains and orchards stretch out between rocky hills, frequently marking the site of an ancient settlement.

The main city in the area is **Castelo Branco** (White Castle). It has been invaded by the Spanish so often that little of historical interest survives. All the same, it is a pleasant city, with small cobbled alleyways leading up to the ruined 'White Castle' at the highest point of the town. The Paço Episcopal ('Palace of the Bishop') is now home to the regional museum, displaying a splendid collection of highly elaborate locally made *colchas* (bedspreads), as well as 16th-century tapestries. The elegant formal Palace Gardens are laid out with an array of baroque statues, sculpted hedges, fountains and pools. The nearby Miradouro de São Gens affords a good view of the city.

The atmospheric village of **Monsanto,** located about 50km (31 miles) to the northeast of Castelo Branco, balances on a dramatic rocky outcrop amongst great boulders. The streets are too narrow for cars, but a short walk to the castle at the top is worth the effort for the impressive stonework and the view. A beautiful, but roofless, 13th-century Romanesque church can also be seen. A new pousada has just opened here.

Idanha-a-Velha is located on the plains, just between Castelo Branco and Monsanto. It, too, is an ancient village, and was once the Roman town of Igaeditânia, as well as the seat of a Visigothic bishopric. The Romans left walls and a bridge, and the Visigoths a church which, though altered, is still in use.

ESTREMADURA AND RIBATEJO

Estremadura's name derives from the time when 'Portugal' was the territory to the north of the Douro river, and Estremadura (from *extrema Durii*, or 'furthest from the Douro') lay to the extreme south.

The region has an extensive coastline that includes the Costa do Estoril, near Lisbon, with its sophisticated beach resorts and casino. Here, too, are the beautiful historic build-

Between the blue sea and golden sand, you'll find plenty of shade at Nazaré.

ings of scenic Serra da Sintra and the 'Pink Palace' of Queluz. South of the River Tagus (Tejo), the Arrábida peninsula has its own fair share of quiet beaches and rocky hills.

Further north in Estremadura, the coast is wilder, but the pleasant resort and fishing villages of Ericeira, Peniche and Nazaré all provide good swimming and facilities. The region's architectural wonders lie just inland. The gargantuan Convent of Mafra is built on a truly unbelievable scale, while the intimate walled town of Óbidos has an atmosphere all of its own. There is also the impressive Gothic abbey of Alcobaça (the largest in the country), which has played a key role in Portuguese history.

Northeast from the capital, along the Tagus, is the agricultural region of the Ribatejo ('Banks of the Tagus'). Here the highlight is the great city of Tomar, once the headquarters of the Portuguese Knights Templar, whose convent is a must-see. Otherwise the Ribatejo is famous for horses, bulls and bullfighting.

Costa do Estoril and Sintra

The beaches and resorts west of Lisbon are all accessible by train from the capital's Cais do Sodré station. **Estoril**, 29km (18 miles) to the west, is the largest and most chic of the resorts. It has attracted the great and the good since the 18th century, and still has some fine mansions that were originally built for the crowned heads of Europe. The huge **casino** complex, set in the park, is what draws most people these days. The beaches are full of Lisboêtas enjoying a day out, but the water is none too clean. Another big attraction is the old Estoril Golf Club, along with a second club just inland. In late September every year, Estoril reverberates to the roar of racing cars speeding through the streets during the Portuguese Formula 1 Grand Prix.

Locals drawing water from the very impressive Moorish fountain at Sintra.

Just 3km (2 miles) west is the smaller and newer beach resort of **Cascais**, which retains its fishing industry and also houses many Lisbon commuters. The Wednesday fish market is a colourful reminder that tourists do not dominate everything here. For culture, visit the Museu dos Condes de Castro Guimarães, in the Parque Marechal Carmona, on the edge of town. This former palace now holds a museum of archaeological relics, furniture and precious metals.

Further along the coast is **Guincho**, where the water is clean, but very rough. Great Atlantic waves crash on to the beach, creating superb conditions for surfing.

Between Sintra and Lisbon is the elegant rococo-style **Palácio de Queluz**, the pale pink former residence of a number of Portuguese royals, including the afflicted Maria I. The palace is still used today for entertaining visiting dignitaries. The Throne Room is a sumptuous display of gold and glass, and the gardens, once home to a royal zoo, are nowadays full of clipped geometric hedges and lakes, as well as a canal lined with 18th-century *azulejos*. The old kitchen has been converted into a fine restaurant (see p.190) and a new pousada opened at Queluz in 1995.

Sintra, 30km (18 miles) to the northwest of Lisbon, is set amongst a series of cool verdant hills, and over the years has attracted royalty, tourists and writers alike. Lord Byron, though generally unimpressed with Portugal, thought Sintra a paradise. The Palácio Nacional (or Paço Real) lies in the centre of the town and was a royal summer retreat for six centuries. Its strange conical chimneys lend the 14th–16th-century exterior a whimsical appearance, while the interior is a wonderful blend of styles. The green and blue *azulejo* tiles of the Sala dos Arabes recall the time when Sintra was a Moorish centre. The painted ceilings are particularly impressive, and the one in the Sala das Pêgas depicts 136 painted magpies. These represent the gossiping ladies-in-waiting to Queen Philippa, one of whom King João I was seen 'innocently' kissing. The bird theme continues in the Manueline Sala dos Cisnes, where 27 painted swans swim across the ceiling.

A very enjoyable, if somewhat strenuous, walk takes you through what looks like a primeval forest, covered with ferns, up to the ruined **Castelo dos Mouros** (Castle of the Moors) that sits impressively on a ridge of rock overlooking the town. From its crenellated walls there are sweeping views in every direction.

Just up from the castle is the **Palácio da Pena**, a weird and wonderful folly that would look more at home in Mad King Ludwig's Bavaria. It was indeed built by a German, Ferdinand II, consort of Queen Maria II. Constructed in 1840, it is a bizarre mix of Gothic, Scottish Baronial, Moorish, Manueline and Renaissance styles. The interior is a similar riot of influences, with a genuine cloister and chapel from the original monastery that stood on the site before the 1755 earthquake.

Other sites in the area include the rather curious corklined cells of the **Convento dos Capuchos** and the elegant Palácio de Seteais, now a hotel (see p.182). 6km (3 miles) to the west is the pretty hill village of **Colares**, best known for its fine red wine, and another 10km (6 miles) on is the rugged coastline at Cabo da Roca, the westernmost point of the European mainland.

South of the Tagus

The journey across the awe-inspiring **Ponte 25 de Abril** suspension bridge over the Tagus provides you with a marvellous view over the hills of Lisbon and, to the south, of the massive Statue of Christ the King, cousin to the famous Rio statue.

The beaches of the **Costa da Caparica**, 6km (3 miles) west of the bridge, are popular with Portuguese tourists, especially since the water is clean. The long half-moon-shaped bays go on for miles. During the summer a narrow-gauge railway runs along the coast, stopping at each of the 20 resorts on the route.

The principal north-south highway runs south from the bridge and passes close to the scenic castle at **Palmela** (after 36km/22 miles). The town's long history goes back to the Romans and continues today in the pousada (see p.182) located in the monastery inside the walls. On a clear day, the views from the castle stretch to Lisbon, the Alentejo and as far as Setúbal.

Setúbal is 6km (4 miles) further south, a busy city on the Sado estuary and a major fishing and industrial centre. Despite this there is plenty to see, notably the 15th-century

Igreja de Jesus, designed by Diogo Boytac, architect of the vast Jerónimos Monastery in Belém (see p.102). This may well have been the very first Manueline-style building in Portugal (see p.10). Its decoration includes typically Manueline nautical motifs, such as ropes carved in stone and twisting into columns. There are also some very fine 17th-century *azulejos*.

The adjoining cloister now houses the town museum, with a collection of archaeological finds and restored Portuguese and Flemish paintings of the 15th and 16th centuries. On a ridge above the town lies a 16th-century fortress, recently converted into a pousada. Ferries depart from Setúbal for the beaches of the Tróia Peninsula (see p.113).

At festival time streets can be strewn with flowers or roofed with streamers, as here in Setúbal.

West from Setúbal, the landscape is dominated by the precipitous **Serra da Arrábida** mountain range, which runs for some 35km (22 miles) and reaches up to 500m (1,650ft) in height. **Vila Nogueira de Azeitão** is worth a visit for the two Fonseca wineries and the tasty local cheese.

The resort of **Sesimbra** has managed to avoid excessive development and has kept its fishing boats and way of life. Sailing, fishing and diving are popular pastimes. High above the harbour is the Moorish castle, whose views warrant the steep walk. Further west is the lonely Cabo Espichel, which juts out into the Atlantic and is home to a pilgrimage sanctuary.

Southern Estremadura

The great monument in this area is the massive **Palace-Convent of Mafra**, 29 km (18 miles) north of Queluz. The gigantic neoclassical complex was started in 1717 to celebrate the birth of João V's heir. The architect was the German, Friedrich Ludwig (who also redesigned Évora's cathedral; see p.105). The convent took 13 years to build, and 45,000 people worked on it at any one time. Its huge cost gave rise to the saying that João transformed the diamonds of Brazil into the rocks of Mafra.

The Royal Apartments consist of a series of painted rooms, all in a row, with one side for the king and the other for the queen. Hunting was a favourite royal pastime, as is immediately obvious from the Sala dos Troféus ('Trophy Room'), where nearly everything is made from antlers and deer skin.

The convent part of Mafra includes a very long hall, with monks' cells off to the side, and a hospital with a special room for self-fla-

The neoclassical interior of the great Mafra Convent, completed at vast expense.

PORTUGUESE WRITERS

The Portuguese have an especially strong feeling for poetry, but their writers have produced fine prose works as well. All the works listed below are available in English translation.

Gil Vicente (1470-1536): Manuel I's court playwright wrote not only comedies but also history and poetry. His plays are frequently performed in Lisbon.

Luís de Camões (1524-80): the great poet of the Age of Discoveries was shipwrecked off the coast of Southeast Asia but survived to complete *The Lusiads*, his epic poem telling of Vasco de Gama's pioneering voyage to India.

Almeida Garrett (1799-1854): a Romantic poet, essayist and playwright whose *Travels in My Homeland* is a semi-autobiographical account of life, love and travels in the Ribatejo during the period of the War of the Brothers (see p.24).

José Maria Eça de Queiroz (1845-1900): the country's greatest novelist showed his Dickens-like concern for social reform in novels like *The Maias* and *The Crime of Father Amaro*.

Fernando Pessoa (1888-1935): this brilliant modernist poet wrote under many pseudonyms. His classic work is *Mensagem (Message)*, and a statue shows him seated at work outside the A Brasileira café, in the Chiado district of Lisbon (see p.101).

José Saramago (1922-): this inventive novelist won prizes for his *Memorial do Convento* (published in English under the title *Blimunda and Baltasar*), which tells the twin story of Mafra (see p.83) and the monk/inventor Padre Gusmão (see p.66). *The Year of the Death of Ricardo Reis* tells the unusual story of the ghost of Fernando Pessoa (see above).

gellation, conveniently near a doctor. The crowning glory is
the magnificent 84m (276ft) library, with its white barrel-
vaulted ceiling. It contains 40,000 books, and competes with
the Coimbra University Library (see p.65) as the finest in
Portugal.

The Renaissance-style basilica is located in the centre
of the complex, and was constructed using marble from all
over Portugal. The church contains no less than six organs.
The belltowers enclose 114 bells and a unique carillon, recently renovated by the same Flemish firm that originally
built it in the 18th century.

Just to the west of Mafra (10km/6 miles) is the popular
coastal resort and fishing town of **Ericeira**. The buildings of
the town are attractively whitewashed and there are plenty of
cafés and hotels. You'll find the best beaches to the north, including some that are famous for their surfing.

About 30km (18 miles) to the north is **Torres Vedras**,
where Wellington built a series of earthworks in secret to
frustrate the French armies during the Peninsular War. The
'lines' are not easy to retrace, but there is a reconstructed fort
outside town and the British Historical Society of Portugal
produces a pamphlet explaining the site.

Northern Estremadura

The magical walled town of **Óbidos**, 37km (23 miles) to the
north of Torres Vedras, once stood on the coast, until a lagoon
formed and stranded it 10km (6 miles) from the sea. Traditionally the town was given as a wedding gift from the King
of Portugal to his bride. The crenellated town walls allow you
to walk all the way round the town, looking down on the picturesque gardens, houses and alleyways. A powerful castle
sits at one end of the town, now converted into a luxurious
pousada (see p.183). Nearby is the splendid Igreja de Santa

Maria, on the town square, decorated with blue and white *azulejos*. The town museum, run by the Gulbenkian Foundation, is also worth a look, especially for its fascinating explanation of the comings and goings of the Peninsular War.

The old fishing village of **Peniche** (22km/14 miles west) also experienced a dramatic change in its coastline, being transformed from an island into a peninsula. The harbour is the centre of activity, with its brightly coloured trawlers and excellent fish restaurants. Pirates (often English) were a persistent problem here during the Spanish occupation, hence the defensive walls, now decaying, and the 16th-century fort, which now houses a museum featuring the dark side of the Salazar regime. The best beach is on the northern side of the peninsula.

The tiny island of **Berlenga** (10km/6 miles away by boat) makes an excellent day trip from Peniche (summers only). The island has a fort and a monastery, and is of particular interest to naturalists, being home to thousands of wonderful seabirds.

For really fresh fish, Peniche is the place to come – watch the fishermen sorting their catch.

North of Óbidos (32km/20 miles) is the colossal monastery of **Alcobaça**, the largest church in Portugal. Like Batalha (see p.71), it was built to celebrate a victory in war. In this case its construction was ordered by Afonso I after his capture of Santarém from the Moors in 1147. The Cistercian order took over and became increasingly wealthy and powerful, until the banning of all religious orders in 1834. The spacious church dates mostly from the 13th century, with various additions from subsequent centuries. The highlights are the two beautifully carved tombs of King Pedro I and Inês de Castro, his Spanish lover, who was cruelly murdered on the orders of Pedro's father, Afonso IV. When Pedro himself came to the throne in 1357, he claimed that he and Inês had been secretly married in Bragança, and took his revenge on her killers, earning him the sobriquet 'the Justicer' (*o Justiceiro*).

> When visiting churches, do not wear shorts, backless dresses or tank tops.

The 14th-century cloisters and elegant chapterhouse are other sights not to be missed. Also be sure to visit the large 18th-century kitchen, where a small diverted stream runs right through to provide water and a highly effective waste-disposal system.

Nazaré (Nazareth), about 14km (8 miles) northwest of Alcobaça, used to be a very scenic fishing village. Recent development has changed its way of life, and the construction of a new harbour means that the sight of men pulling their colourful small boats on to the sands is much rarer. Even so, many in the town still earn their living from fishing, and you will see old women, wearing the traditional seven layers of petticoats, drying their fish on racks down by the beach. The clifftop district of **Sítio**, at the northern end of the beach, has fine views and many quiet holiday villas for rent.

It can be reached by means of a funicular railway that climbs the 110m (360ft) cliff face.

☛ The Ribatejo

Santarém, 78km (48 miles) northeast of Lisbon, is the ancient capital of the agricultural region of the Ribatejo, whose lifeblood is the mighty River Tagus. The city was named after St Iria, the 7th-century martyr, and served as a Moorish centre until it was captured by Afonso I in 1147.

Few of Santarém's monuments have survived, although the Jesuit seminary and church on the main square, the triangular Largo Sá da Bandeira, has a very impressive 17th-century baroque façade. To the north of the city centre you'll find the 15th-century Graça church, with its magnificent Gothic rose window, amazingly carved from a single piece of stone. In the south of the city is the Marvila church, built in Manueline style, with its fine 17th-century *azulejos* (currently under renovation) and the Cabaças Tower, fairly plain except for the eight unusual clay pots on the top. Across the street is an interesting archaeological museum in a Romanesque church, guarded by two stone elephants.

The finest view in town is from the Portas do Sol, a garden surrounded by Moorish walls overlooking the River Tagus and the extensive plains of the Ribatejo. A Phoenician dye house has recently been discovered in the grounds.

Bulls and horses can be seen grazing all over the Ribatejo. Santarém is the centre for dressage and **Vila Franca de Xira** (45km/28 miles down the Tagus in the direction of Lisbon) the mecca for bullfighting. Every July and October Pamplona-style bull running accompanies the bullfights. Many of the horses used here come from **Golegã**, where the National Horse Fair is held every November.

Numerous migratory birds can be seen in the Tagus Estuary Natural Reserve, whose headquarters is in **Alcochete**.

Tomar (34km/21 miles east of Fátima), sitting astride the River Nabão, is one of Portugal's most fascinating cities. Its pleasant central plaza is flanked by the very elegant Manueline church of São João Baptista, with an unusual octagonal belfry, and the 17th-century town hall. The real story of the town, though, is to be found in the statue in the centre of the plaza. It depicts Gualdim Pais, Grand Master of the Portuguese branch of the crusading Knights Templar, to whom the town was granted in 1157.

The Templars' old stronghold, the Castelo dos Templários (Templars' Castle) and the accompanying Convento do Cristo (Convent of Christ), both overlook Tomar from the

The intriguing, rather strange castle complex
of the Knights Templar in Tomar.

wooded heights to the west of the city. Here you will find a whole complex of medieval buildings, surrounded by crenellated walls enclosing formal gardens and protected by a small keep (the latter is closed to the public).

At the heart of the complex is the interesting 12th-century Charola, a 16-sided structure loosely based on the Church of the Holy Sepulchre (built over Christ's tomb) in Jerusalem. The knights used to attend the services here on horseback! Restoration is currently under way to bring back to life some of its esoteric paintings. The two-storied nave, added by Manuel I, is divided into an upstairs choir and a chapterhouse underneath. One of the finest Manueline windows in Portugal is to be found in the wall of the chapterhouse, encrusted with carved marine motifs. Several cloisters were added at a later date, including the spacious Renaissance-style Claustro Principal.

Unusually, for a town so dominated by Christian crusaders, a small 15th-century synagogue survives. The room has a high groin-vaulted ceiling, along with eight clay pots embedded in the walls to improve the acoustics (classical concerts are now held here). A museum displays old tombstones. In 1992, Yom Kippur was celebrated here for the first time in 500 years.

From Tomar there is a fine excursion to the fairytale castle at **Almourol**, sitting on an island in the Tagus and once a Templar stronghold. Just upriver you will find the rather picturesque town of **Abrantes** with its own castle.

 LISBON

Portugal's capital city is by far the country's largest, with a population of more than 2 million. Despite this, the place is rarely oppressive, and has the cosmopolitan atmosphere of a lived-in historic centre. Old sections of the town survive in the winding alleys of the medieval and Moorish district, known as the Alfama, though this is for the most part a city of 18th-century architecture. Large areas were razed flat by the massive earthquake of 1755 and the city was subsequently rebuilt with money from the colonies. (The city is covered in more detail in the Berlitz POCKET GUIDE TO LISBON).

> **Underground fare in Lisbon is the same irrespective of the distance you travel.**

The River Tagus (Tejo) meanders among Lisbon's many hills, and is the reason for the city's development and importance. The hills divide the city into distinct areas, each with its own character and atmosphere, ranging from the wide boulevards of the Baixa, to the small, intimate squares and *fado* houses of the Bairro Alto, and the dominating heights of the Castelo de São Jorge (St George's Castle).

Binding all this together are the friendly people of Lisbon (affectionately known as *alfacinhas*, or 'little cabbages') who passionately love their city and welcome visitors who share their enthusiasm.

Old Lisbon and the East

The medieval **Alfama** district spills down the side of a hill between the Castelo de São Jorge and the Tagus with all the colour and bustle of an Arab bazaar. Its knot of tiny streets can really only be experienced on foot, but do expect to get lost and don't bring valuables. Most of the 12,000 or so people who live here are very friendly and busily go about their daily routine of selling fish or washing clothes. Hidden away amongst the intricate maze of alleys are several beautiful small squares and churches, such as the octagonal 13th-century **Igreja de Santo Estêvão** or the impressively restored Igreja de São Miguel. Many people consider the Alfama to be the most atmospheric part of Lisbon, especially since it

was one of the few areas to survive the earthquake, so that it retains its ancient Moorish character. You will find this reflected in the haunting sound of the Arabic-influenced *fado* music (see p.131), which is at its most authentic here.

The ramparts of the Moorish **Castelo de São Jorge** give a great view over Lisbon. They also enclose pleasant gardens, home to many exotic birds. The fall of the castle to crusaders in 1147 proved crucial in the Reconquest of Portugal from the Moors. The district round the castle is known as the Mouraria ('Moorish Quarter') and is, with the Alfama, Lisbon's oldest.

Further down the hill is the squat Romanesque form of the **Sé** (Cathedral). Its fortress-like exterior is similar to those of Oporto and Coimbra, and like them it dates from the 12th-century, right in the middle of the Reconquest. Various bits and pieces have been added over the years, but the interest-

One of the capital's most fascinating museums is the ever-colourful Azulejo Museum (above). Lisbon's cathedral (right).

ing features are the sentimental 14th-century tombs and the medieval cloister.

Also near the castle is the large Renaissance church of **São Vicente de Fora**, whose small *azulejo*-lined cloister is worth a look. The **Pantheon of Santa Engrácia** lies just down the hill. Now a secular building, dedicated to the great figures of Portuguese history, its impressive high dome was originally constructed to cover a church. Between the two is the **Campo de Santa Clara**, where the capital's best flea market (the ominously named Feira da Ladra, 'Thief's Market') takes place every Tuesday and Saturday. Everything can be found here, from complete junk to quality antiques and rare books. Nearby is the **Military Museum** (see p.96) and **Santa Apolonia** railway station (the point of departure for trains to the north).

Further east along the riverfront is the marvellous **Madre de Deus** convent, home to the **Azulejo Museum** (see p.96)

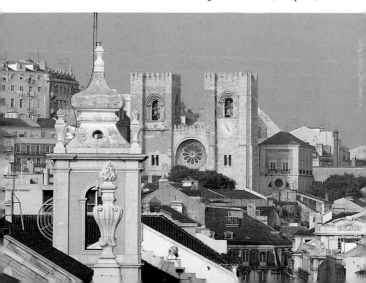

LISBON'S MUSEUMS

Lisbon's museums are generally open 10am to 5pm (some stay open to 6pm or 6.30pm in summer). They close every Monday and for lunch from 12.30pm or 1pm until 2pm or 2.30pm. Entrance costs between 50 and 500 escudos, but is often free on Sunday. Ask at the tourist office (see p.171) for details of special exhibitions.

Ancient Art Museum (Museu Nacional de Arte Antiga), *Rua das Janelas Verdes*. European and Portuguese paintings, jewellery, ceramics and sculpture. Bus 27 from Pombal or Belém.

Archaeological Museum (Museu Nacional de Arqueología), *Praça do Império, Belém*. Exhibits from the Stone Age to Roman times, including an important ancient jewellery collection. Tram 15 or 17 from Praça do Comércio; bus 27 from Pombal.

Azulejos (Museu do Azulejo), *Convento de Madre de Deus*. Huge collection of tiles, ancient and modern. Bus 59 from Praça Figuera.

City Museum (Museu da Cidade), *Campo Grande 245*. The history of Lisbon from its origins to 1910. Bus 27 from Pombal.

Coach Museum (Museu dos Coches), *Praça Afonso de Albuquerque, Belém*. Royal coaches and assorted memorabilia. Transport as for Archaeological Museum.

Decorative Arts (Museu Escola de Artes Decorativas), *Largo Portas do Sol 2, Alfama*. Furniture, metal, pottery and weaving from different periods. Tram 28 from Baixa.

Folk Art (Museu de Arte Popular), *Avenida Brasília, Belém*. Various folk arts and crafts. Transport as for Archaeological Museum.

Gulbenkian Museum (Museu Calouste Gulbenkian), *Avenida de Berna 45*. Excellent collection of fine works of art. Good Islamic collection. Also a separate Modern Art Museum across the park. Metro São Sebastião; bus 31, 41 or 46 from Rossio or Pombal.

Military Museum (Museu Militar), *Largo dos Caminhos de Ferro*. Old weapons and armour. Bus 12 from Pombal.

Naval Museum (Museu da Marinha), *Praça do Império, Belém*. Tells the story of the great Age of the Discoveries through models of ships. Transport as for Archaeological Museum.

and further still lies the site of the **1998 World Expo**, whose oceanic theme celebrates the 500th anniversary of Vasco de Gama's great voyage to India.

The Centre and the North

The entire area between the hills of Castelo de São Jorge and the Bairro Alto, a district known as the **Baixa** ('Lowland'), was devastated by the great earthquake of 1755. This gave the Marquês de Pombal, who supervised the city's reconstruction, the opportunity to redesign the area, based on a geometric system of broad avenues. Pombal was a great rationalist and set aside streets for each of the main professions, as evidenced by names such as Rua dos Douradores (Gilders' Street) and Rua dos Fanqueiros (Drapers' Street).

The area's main square, the particularly impressive **Praça do Comércio** (also called by its former name of the Terreiro do Paço) opens out on one side to the Tagus riverbank (the Ribeira). To the English inhabitants of Lisbon,

Shadows lock together as a cavaleiro demonstrates his skill in a tourada.

The Mercado da Ribeira is the city's most atmospheric market.

this is known as Black Horse Square, on account of the fine equestrian statue of José I, who was on the throne at the time of the city's rebuilding.

Ferries ply across the Tagus from a point near the square, and from another to the west, near the **Cais do Sodré** railway station, the place to catch trains for Estoril and Cascais. To experience the real life of Lisbon, visit the **Mercado da Ribeira**, the principal produce market, to watch the colourful hawkers and purchase the ingredients for a picnic.

A wide pedestrian shopping street, the **Rua Augusta**, leads from the Praça do Comércio through a stately arch to the central square of Lisbon, the **Rossio** (the Common). Once the scene of bullfights, it now hosts a funfair and is a popular meeting point, ringed by cafés. The National Theatre is here, and across the road is the Rossio station (trains to Sintra), with its double-horseshoe doorway in a mix of Manueline and Indian styles.

Another main square, the **Praça da Figueira**, sits just next door, graced by a statue of João I. This is where many bus and tram routes start, and period tickets can be purchased from the Carris Office here.

Just up from the Rossio is the **Praça dos Restauradores** (Square of the Restorers), with its obelisk commemorating the overthrow of Spanish Habsburg rule in 1640. The main **tourist office** is here at Palácio Foz, on the west side of the square.

The very broad and leafy Avenida da Liberdade runs for 1km (0.6 mile) north, flanked by gardens, ponds and fountains, as far as the circular **Praça Marquês de Pombal** (also known as the Rotunda), where a statue of the fearless Pombal and a lion gaze over his recreated city. Many airlines have offices around here.

The Praça dos Restauradores celebrates the end of Spanish rule in 1640.

The pleasant, immaculately laid out **Parque Eduardo VII** runs north from Pombal, and provides a peaceful place to stretch your legs near the centre of the city. The name recalls a visit by the English King Edward VII in 1903. For a taste of exotic botany, visit the Estufa Fria (Cold Greenhouse) in a corner of the park. It houses tropical plants from all over the world, recalling Portugal's time as the ruler of a worldwide empire.

Just to the north of Parque Eduardo VII are the **Lisbon City Museum** and Portugal's finest art collection, housed in the **Gulbenkian Museum** (see p.96 for both museums). A little further

The poet Fernando Pessoa still frequents his favourite café in the Chiado district.

north is the impressive 18th-century **Aguas Livres Aqueduct**, which still carries water along its 18km (11 mile) length to a point near the modern Amoreiras Shopping Centre.

Bairro Alto

High on a hill to the west of the Baixa is the **Bairro Alto** (Upper District), home to picturesque squares, antiquarian bookshops, *fado* houses, small restaurants, lively bars and the **Port Wine Institute** (Solar do Vinho do Porto, Rua de São Pedro de Alcântara 45). An easy way of reaching the Bairro Alto is to take one of the funicular trolleys that run from behind the Praça dos Restauradores and the Praça de Camões (near the Cais do Sodre). On the other hand, the **Elevador Santa Justa** (which opened in 1902), offers a more scenic route and transports you up from the Baixa to the Largo do Carmo.

Here you'll find one of Lisbon's most evocative sights, the shell of the 14th-century **Igreja do Carmo**, which was packed with worshippers on All Saints' Day, 1755, when the terrible earthquake brought down the roof. It now houses an interesting archaeological museum. Another church well worth a visit is the **Igreja de São Roque**. Whilst this certainly does not look like much from the outside, the interior houses the incredibly lavish baroque chapel of São João Baptista (St John the Baptist), with its extraordinary treasure trove of valuable stones. Next door along you'll find a small **Museum of Sacred Art**.

From the **Miradouro de São Pedro de Alcântara** there is a pleasant view across to the Castelo de São Jorge. Nearby are a number of good antique shops and the tranquil **Jardim Botânico** (Botanical Garden). Running down the hill to the Tagus is the elegant shopping district of the **Chiado**. Devastated by fire in 1988, this has been rebuilt and is still the top place to shop in Portugal.

Just west of the Bairro Alto is the affluent Estrêla (Star) district, with an enjoyable park set beside the large **Basilica de Estrêla**. From the dome of the basilica there are marvellous views. Also in Estrêla is the **English Church**, St. George's, and its cemetery (ring for admittance), where the novelist Henry Fielding lies amongst many evocative old tombs.

Belém

A short way along the Tagus, 6km (4 miles) west of the city centre, is Belém (Portuguese for Bethlehem), from where many of the great voyages of discovery set out in the 15th and 16th centuries. Fittingly it is also the setting for two great examples of Manueline architecture (see p.10) and a **Naval Museum** (see p.96).

Construction of the massive **Mosteiro dos Jerónimos** was begun by Manuel I. It was designed in the Manueline style that became so popular during his reign. The convent itself did not survive the 1755 earthquake, but the amazing church and cloister remain, both displaying fine Manueline detail in the motifs of twisted stone ropes and anchors.

The other typically Manueline building to be found in Belém is the small and intricate **Torre de Belém**, which sits just offshore, surrounded by water. Its particularly intriguing ship-like outline commonly features on Portuguese tourist posters.

Also along the shoreline here is the modern **Padrão dos Descobrimentos** (Monument to the Discoveries), a curious structure sticking out over the water and supporting statues of Henry the Navigator and Camões, the great Portuguese poet. A large inlaid stone map is set into the ground in front, tracing the routes of the great Portuguese explorers.

Belém is home to a profusion of museums – the best of which are listed on p.96. Other attractions are the Gulbenkian Institute's **Planetarium** and the huge **Centro Cultural de Belém**, opened in 1992 when Portugal assumed the presidency of the EEC (now the European Union), and today hosting concerts and shows.

North of Belém is the 19th-century **Palácio da Ajuda** which, like the Pena Palace in Sintra (see p.80), was built at the behest of Maria II and her German consort, Ferdinand. While not as fantastical as the Pena Palace, its sumptuous interior verges on the gaudy, and the banqueting hall alone is well worth the tour.

*The Alentejo produces much
of the world's cork (above) and
more tasty products (left).*

ALENTEJO

The 'Land beyond the Tagus' (*alem Tejo* in Arabic) is the hot
and dusty plain, covered in olive and cork trees, that many
tourists drive through between Lisbon and the Algarve,
oblivious to the fact they are crossing one of the most interesting regions in the country.

Although the Alentejo accounts for approximately one
third of Portugal's land area, it is fairly sparsely populated,
and the inhabitants are traditionally the butt of Portuguese
jokes (such as the one about the Alentejano who keeps an
empty bottle in the fridge for his friends who don't drink). In
fact, the Alentejo is far more sophisticated and varied than it
first appears, and Évora is one of Portugal's finest historic
cities. Massive medieval fortresses sit atop steep hills guarding the Spanish border, and ancient megalithic standing

stones dot the countryside. The Alentejo even has its own *costa*: the Costa Azul, or Blue Coast, a lower-key version of the Algarve.

☞ Évora

Évora is a definite must-see, and could take days to explore fully, though tour companies arrange day trips from the Algarve and Lisbon (the city is 150km/93 miles east of Lisbon and 257km/159 miles north of Faro). Originally a Roman settlement, Évora is now a city of attractive Renaissance buildings, mostly dating from its great heyday as the base of the House of Aviz, rulers of Portugal from the 14th century until the Spanish Habsburgs took over in 1581. At this point, Évora became a backwater and development came to a halt, thus preserving the city's distinctive 16th-century *palácios* for posterity.

Évora is a marvellous place to just wander around; this is the Largo da Porto da Moura.

Town walls helpfully enclose all the sights. Amongst the great maze of Moorish alleys are numerous large and small squares (*praças*) which are handy to use as reference points. You'll find the tourist office on the ever-busy **Praça do Giraldo**.

Another useful point of orientation is the unmistakable **Templo Romano** (or Roman Temple), sometimes called the Temple of Diana, though current research suggests rather that it was a temple to Jupiter. Its 14 Corinthian columns sit atop a platform which was still in use in the 19th century as a slaughterhouse.

Right next to the Temple is the very elegant **Pousada dos Lóios** (see p.185), formerly a convent. If you are not staying there, it is worth a visit, especially for the two-tier cloister. Abutting the pousada is the privately owned church of **São João Evangelista** (also known as Lóios, the old church of the same convent). It has one of the country's finest examples of *azulejo* tilework, created in the 18th century by the celebrated artist, Antônio Oliveira Bernardes, and depicting the tale of São Lourenço (St Lawrence). The church holds several more surprises, such as the Moorish cistern, 15m (50ft) deep and hidden under a trapdoor on one side of the aisle, the collection of monks' bones in the ossuary under the other trapdoor, and the confession holes that open onto the pousada's cloister, whence you can spy on diners.

The nearby **Sé** (Cathedral) betrays its crusading origins in its fortress-like Romanesque style. Note the statues of the Twelve Apostles by the door and their odd gargoyle friends. The impressive eastern wing was rebuilt by Friedrich Ludwig, the architect of the Convent at Mafra (see p.83), using the multicoloured marble of the Alentejo. Be sure not to miss the especially beautiful Gothic cloister and the Sacred Art Museum, with its impressive collection of relics and clerical vestments.

Another fascinating, if a little chilling church, is that of **São Fransisco**, with its Capela dos Ossos (Bone Chapel). In this gruesome room, the bones of 5,000 monks have been used as architectural building blocks, so that skulls form the window frames and leg bones cover the columns. The 'ashes to ashes, dust to dust' theme is completed by a sign that

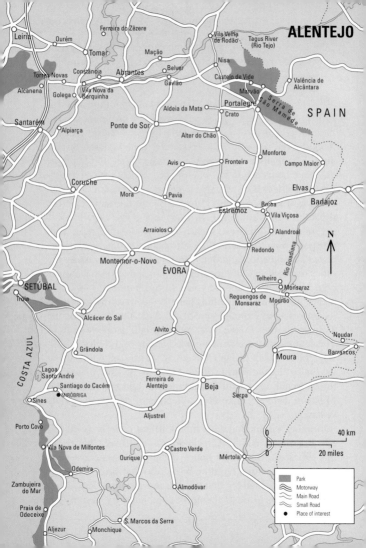

reads: '*Nós ossos que aqui estamos, Pelos vossos esperamos*' ('We bones that are here, await the coming of your bones').

The **Municipal Museum**, not far from the cathedral, is housed in the old archbishop's palace and displays an important collection of paintings by the Flemish-inspired 'Portuguese School', the finest of these being the 13 panels depicting the *Life of the Virgin*. The museum also contains an eclectic mix of stone sculptures, including some Roman tombstones, several Arab votive inscriptions, and medieval tomb carvings.

The fine town of **Arraiolos**, 21km (13 miles) to the north of Évora, makes a good day trip and is famed for its carpet workshops. Carpets, in the Moorish-Persian style, have been made here ever since the 17th century. They are expensive (though cheaper here than elsewhere) but very beautiful.

Another excellent day trip from Évora is to the megaliths near **Reguengos de Monsaraz** (36km/22 miles to the southeast). These slightly baffling prehistoric monuments consist of standing stones (menhirs) and stone circles (cromlechs) that would not look out of place in Ireland or Britanny (ask the tourist office in Évora for precise directions).

Near the Spanish border is the stunning fortified hilltop village of **Monsaraz**. Its

Whitewashed buildings are that little bit cooler during the Alentejo's fierce summer.

cobbled streets are very quiet and the views over the plains, with the ever-present cork and olive trees, are spectacular. The castle (now housing a bullring) is one in the long chain of fortifications built by Dom Dinis in the 14th century.

The Marble Towns and Elvas

About 46km (28 miles) northeast of Évora, marble replaces more mundane building materials for churches and palaces, thanks to the great number of quarries at Estremoz, Borba and Vila Viçosa.

The largest of these quarries is near **Estremoz**, a walled town full of marble gleaming white above the plains. The Rossio (Praça Marquês de Pombal) forms the heart of the lower town and is home to the lively Saturday market, where you can buy the famous pottery of Estremoz, tasty local cheese, and any of the other agricultural products of the Alentejo. There is a tourist office on the square, as well as an interesting Rural Museum (Museu Rural) displaying a wealth of idiosyncratic local gadgets and pottery. Also here is the beautiful marble-faced Town Hall (Câmara Municipal), converted from an old convent with impressive *azulejo* panels.

The upper town is reached through medieval walls, and is where you'll find the castle's Keep, visible for miles around and giving great views over the region. Inside the Keep is the *azulejo*-covered chapel of Rainha Santa Isabel, dedicated to the memory of Dom Dinis' sainted queen. To one side of the Keep is the white-marble Royal Palace, now one of the country's best pousadas.

Borba, on the road to Elvas and Spain, is a more down-to-earth town, though its marble buildings betray the source of the local wealth: the people of Borba make their living from extracting marble from quarries, as well as producing fine red and white wines.

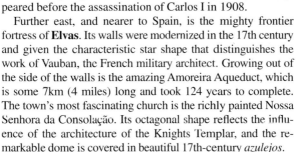

Just 6 km (4 miles) away is the third marble town, **Vila Viçosa**. This one contains the very impressive 16th-century Ducal Palace (Paço Ducal) of the Bragança family, the last of Portugal's royal dynasties. It used to be the favourite country house of the family, who often preferred hunting in the enormous park to all the fuss of Lisbon or the cold of their palace in Bragança (see p.58). The guided tour provides an intimate glimpse of the apartments as they would have appeared before the assassination of Carlos I in 1908.

Further east, and nearer to Spain, is the mighty frontier fortress of **Elvas**. Its walls were modernized in the 17th century and given the characteristic star shape that distinguishes the work of Vauban, the French military architect. Growing out of the side of the walls is the amazing Amoreira Aqueduct, which is some 7km (4 miles) long and took 124 years to complete. The town's most fascinating church is the richly painted Nossa Senhora da Consolação. Its octagonal shape reflects the influence of the architecture of the Knights Templar, and the remarkable dome is covered in beautiful 17th-century *azulejos*.

Northeastern Alentejo

Portalegre is the no-nonsense capital of the northern Alentejo, located near the hills and neolithic monuments of the Serra de São Mamede, 59 km (36 miles) north of Estremoz. Its past wealth, based on carpet and silk production, accounts for the many graceful 18th-century mansions lining the Rua 19 de Junho. By far the most interesting sight in town is the Tapestry Factory (Manufactura de Tapeçarias), housed in a 17th-century Jesuit school, where you can watch dozens of women using great handlooms to weave carpets from thousands of different shades of wool.

Horse fans should be sure to visit **Alter do Chão** (33km/20 miles southeast of Portalegre), the location of

An 18th-century ceiling in Beja.

the Royal Stud Farm (Coudelaria de Alter Real). Here Portugal's finest horses are bred. If you arrive in the morning you can watch the Lusitanian and Alter do Chão horses being fed. There is also an interesting museum, and the town of Alter do Chão itself has a fine restored castle.

North from Portalegre is the pleasant town of **Castelo de Vide**, whose 14th-century castle is surrounded by gleaming houses that nuzzle against the steeply sloping hill. Further down the hill, the winding alleyways of the Judiaria (Jewish Quarter) have survived and make a great place for wandering. Amongst these houses is the country's oldest surviving synagogue (13th-century). For centuries the fresh springs at Fonte de Vila, close to the handsome main square, the Praça Dom Pedro V, have been another of Castelo de Vide's many attractions.

Even lovelier is the dramatic walled village of **Marvão**, just to the east and overlooking Spain. The castle appears woven into the natural rock and gives fantastic views of the area, while the town is a wonderful place to unwind, as life generally moves at a slow pace here.

Lower (Baixo) Alentejo

Being of Roman origin, the agricultural city of **Beja** (about 78km/48 miles to the south of Évora) is at the hub of several roads and so makes a convenient stopping-off point. The decoratively crenellated Torre de Menagem, in the castle, provides a good lookout over the extensive wheatfields of the southern Alentejo.

The city's most interesting sight is the Convento de Nossa Senhora da Conceição, with its fine Manueline carving, bright *azulejos* and an explosion of rococo gold leaf. Nowadays the convent houses an interesting regional museum with a good archaeological and painting collection. There is also a unique Visigothic Art Museum in the small church of Santo Amaro, close by the castle. The new Pousada de São Fransisco has been admirably converted from another convent, once derelict.

The charming, sleepy town of **Serpa** rises neatly above the plains, 30km (18 miles) east of Beja, on the route to Spain. Small streets wind in and out among the bright white houses. Many of the buildings hide small cheese factories, which produce Serpa's famous ewes' milk cheese. The town's castle was partially destroyed by a Spanish attack in 1707 but still affords enjoyable views. The walls continue

The walled village of Marvão offers sweeping views of the rugged countryside.

Mértola (above) dates back to Roman times.

past a privately owned 17th-century mansion and on to a slender aqueduct, which ends in an ancient well with a working chain-pulley system for drawing water. A small ethnographic museum displays the wares of the agricultural and industrial workers of the area.

From Serpa there is a rewarding drive south towards the eastern Algarve, through a hilly and sparsely populated landscape where you will see shepherds tending their flocks. Along the way is **Mértola**, perched on a ridge at the junction of the River Guadiana and the smaller Oeiras. The town is protected by Moorish walls and topped by a rather dilapidated castle with a profusion of storks' nests.

Mértola is full of history: its church, the Igreja Matriz, betrays a previous incarnation as a mosque with a prayer niche (*mihrab*), while the town hall (now a museum) is constructed on Roman foundations. The Guadiana continues as far as the Algarve, forming part of the border with Spain. The road that follows its banks is one of the most beautiful access routes between the Alentejo and the Algarve.

Coastal Alentejo

The Alentejo coast is a popular holiday destination with the Portuguese and has a character slightly different from that of the Algarve. The water here is colder, and the winds and waves greater, but it is also noticeably quieter, more relaxed and less expensive. Often the best beaches are those near a river estuary, thus giving visitors the choice of surfing in the Atlantic or swimming in the calmer waters of the river.

The northernmost point of the coastal Alentejo is the narrow, sandy peninsula of **Tróia**, 46km (28 miles) northwest of the attractive town of Alcácer do Sal. Tróia has beaches on both the Sado estuary and the ocean, but the town has been heavily developed in recent years to accommodate ferries from Setúbal (see p.82). Even so, it is worth visiting the re-

It's worth taking advantage of the numerous fountains that grace towns in Portugal.

mains of the Roman fishing village of Cetobriga; and you can escape the crowds on the beaches of the ocean side.

Further to the south and slightly inland is the town of **Santiago do Cacém**, hemmed in by low-lying hills on three sides and crowned by a hilltop castle, which holds a macabre cemetery full of disinterred bones. The surrounding hills have a profusion of windmill towers which, without their white canvas sails, look for all the world like ancient cannons. The lagoons of **Santo André** and **Melides** are both easily accessible from Santiago do Cacém and boast long stretches of beach, ocean and lagoon swimming, and small beachside communities.

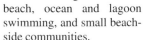

The Algarve's greatest draw is the beach.

On the Lisbon road, just beyond the nearby pousada (see p.185), is the Celto-Roman site of **Miróbriga**, situated in the hills above Santiago do Cacém. The site covers a large area and includes Roman baths as well as a partially reconstructed forum with a temple to Jupiter. A small exhibition beside the entrance explains Miróbriga's place in Roman Portugal (Lusitania).

Further to the south is the main Alentejo beach resort of **Vila Nova de Milfontes**. The River Mira runs past the picturesque town, with its small ivy-covered fortress (now an exclusive guesthouse) and out to the ocean beaches, where there are plenty of apartments for rent. The beaches on the far side of the river, accessible by ferry, are the least crowded.

As you near the Algarve, there are several more small, unobtrusive beach communities, such as **Zambujeira do Mar** and **Almograve**. To arrive at the Algarve, there are two fine routes, one of which continues down the wild and undiscovered west coast (see p.124), while the other passes through the scenic mountains of the Serra de Monchique (see p.123).

THE ALGARVE

To many visitors, the Algarve *is* Portugal, whereas the Portuguese see the Algarve as anything but. The area's distinctive character owes much to its strong Moorish heritage and its Mediterranean climate, so different from most other parts of the country. It is also different because of the huge number of holidaymakers who come to the Algarve compared with the rest of the country – resulting in an explosion of purpose-built holiday villages. Nevertheless, the Algarve does have its quieter areas and also boasts a number of spectacular beaches, a wonderfully sunny climate, and many excellent sporting facilities.

Access from one part of the Algarve to another is made easy by the fast EN125 road, which runs most of the length of the coast, from east to west. The section of coast stretching from Faro eastwards to Spain, known as the Sotavento (Leeward) Coast, is made up of salt marshes and lagoons, with beautiful sandy beaches on the barrier islands just offshore. The most intensively developed part stretches westwards from Faro to Portimão. Here the long beaches are all backed by scores of busy, large-scale tourist resorts.

Albufeira is popular for package holidays.

The more dramatic Barlavento (Windward) Coast extends west from Portimão, and is characterized by a twisting shoreline indented with coves and wind-sculpted cliffs. The coast comes to an end at Cabo São Vicente, known to the Portuguese as the 'end of the world'. From here northward, the west coast of the Algarve is wilder, colder, windier and emptier, though it has its fair share of wonderful beaches. Inland you'll find Roman and Moorish monuments, numerous fruit orchards, and the scenic wooded hillsides of the *serras* that separate the Algarve from the Alentejo.

Faro and the Sotavento Coast

Faro, with its busy international airport, is the Algarve's largest city and the regional capital. Visitors arrive here by plane, but immediately move on to their resorts, so tourism in Faro is not overstated, and relatively relaxed and friendly. The city suffered terribly in the great earthquake of 1755, but some interesting historic buildings have survived.

The **Old Town**, next to the scenic harbour, is surrounded by walls, entered through the large 18th-century gate called the **Arco da Vila** (close by the tourist office). Cobbled streets lead from the gate to the central **Largo da Sé** (Cathedral Square), which is attractively lined with white palaces and orange trees. The **cathedral** itself is a mixture of styles, containing attractive 18th-century *azulejos*. The nearby **Museu Arqueológico e Lapidar** is installed in a lovely 16th-century convent, with magnificent displays of Roman

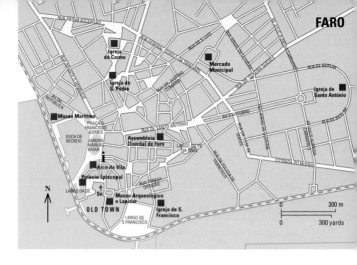

finds, including a very large mosaic of Neptune. The city's strangest sight, however, is the Capela dos Ossos (Bone Chapel), in the impressive baroque **Igreja do Carmo**, which is constructed entirely of human bones, reminiscent of the chapel in Évora (see p.105).

Faro's main beach, the Praia de Faro, is a long sandy spit near the airport, accessible by ferry during the summer from a point near the Largo da Sé. Although the beach has a few hotels and restaurants, it forms part of the Parque Natural da Ria Formosa (see p.118) and has therefore escaped any extreme development.

Inland from Faro there are several historic sites worth visiting. The 18th-century baroque Palácio dos Condes de Carvalhalos, in **Estói**, is similar to the Palace of Queluz (see p.79), though on a smaller scale. It is under renovation, but the impressive gardens are well worth a stroll. From here it is a short walk to the ruins of the Roman villa at **Milreu**,

*Not far from Faro is the baroque
Palácio dos Condes de Carvalhalos.*

where you can see the remains of a temple and mosaics. A relaxing detour 7km (4 miles) further north takes you to the sleepy village of **São Brás de Alportel**, with its colourful market (Saturday). The town's highly interesting Ethnographic Museum gives a good insight into the people of the region and their culture.

The coast east from Faro is dominated by the sandy barrier islands of the **Parque Natural da Ria Formosa**, whose lagoons and mudflats provide a home for many birds and other animals, and a protected location where you can learn to windsurf. **Olhão**, the first town east of Faro, is not particularly scenic, but does boast a very colourful fish market. Ferries run from here to the beaches of Culatra and Armona on the nearby *ilhas* (islands).

One of the prettiest towns in the Algarve is **Tavira**, 30km (18 miles) east of Faro. At its centre is a beautiful collection of churches and flower-filled squares. Tavira once made its living by tuna fishing, and the taste for excellent fresh tuna lingers on. Ferries operate during the summer from the town to the enormous beaches of the **Ilha de Tavira**.

Beyond Tavira, barrier islands begin to give way to modern beach resorts, such as **Cabanas**, **Alagoa** and **Monte Gordo** (the largest) with its enormous hotels and casino. For a quieter village atmosphere, try visiting the undeveloped **Cacela Velha**.

At the eastern edge of the Algarve, facing the Spanish town of Ayamonte across the River Guadiana, is the town of **Vila Real de Santo Antonio**. The town's grid layout is similar to that of the Baixa in Lisbon (see p.97), and likewise it was inspired by the Marquês de Pombal, who created a new town after the earlier one was destroyed by a tidal wave.

Ferries will carry you from Vila Real across the Guadiana to Spain, or you can drive across using the new bridge near **Castro Marim**, 5km (3 miles) north. The huge castle in Castro Marim was once the home of the Knights Templar, who later moved to Tomar (see p.89). The marshes around the town are protected as a nature reserve and make for a pleasant, if muddy, walk.

The River Guadiana itself is one of the most scenic in Portugal and demarcates the border with Spain. Boat trips run upriver from Vila Real to the small agricultural village of **Foz de Odeleite**. From here, you can continue north along the river, through rolling hills and orchards, to the town of **Alcoutim**, where you'll see a compact castle, built largely of slate, and a resplendent white church topped off by a stork's nest. Facing Alcoutim is the Spanish town of **Sanlucar de Guadiana** – easily accessible by passenger ferry – with its own matching fortress, church and storks. The Guadiana then continues up to Mértola in the Alentejo (see p.112).

Central Algarve

The coast between Faro and Portimão has been heavily developed since the revolution of 1974, and here you will find the heaviest concentration of tourists, as well as the best sporting facilities. Just west of Faro is the exclusive resort of **Quinta do Lago**, with its top-class facilities for golf, tennis, watersports and horse-riding. Nearby, but substantially less expensive, is **Vale de Lobo**, with a very good golf course and tennis centre.

Quarteira, 22km (13 miles) west of Faro, was once a fishing village, and some of this local colour has been retained, especially in the busy Wednesday market. Now it is a major tourist resort because of its long and pretty beach.

In contrast, **Vilamoura** was planned from the outset as a giant integrated resort complex of hotels, apartments, golf courses, bars and cafés, not to mention the Algarve's largest marina, bursting with expensive yachts from all over the world. The Romans also had a marina here, remains of which you can see nearby and in the small museum.

For a taste of slightly more traditional Algarvian life, visit **Loulé**, about 11km (7 miles) inland from Quarteira. This is a busy but attractive town, which hosts a highly popular Saturday market and is home to some of the Algarve's finest artisans, who work in leather, clay and copper.

Albufeira (25km/15 miles west of Quarteira) started out as a fishing village and then just grew and grew once tourists started coming. The attraction is the very popular main beach (reached via a tunnel from town), with its strangely shaped sandstone cliffs. The centre of town is packed with lively nightspots, but you can also visit the fish market for an insight into local life. The beaches further to the west of town are just as beautiful and less busy.

A mouth-watering selection of olives tempts passers-by in the town of Loulé.

Porches, 18km (11 miles) west of Albufeira along the EN125, is famed for its pottery and **Lagoa**, 7km (4 miles) further on, is best known for its red and white wines, which are served all over the region. The nearest beach is a short distance south at the charming resort village of **Carvoeiro**.

The Algarve was once an independent Moorish kingdom, with its capital at **Silves** (then called Chelb), 7km (4 miles) north of Lagoa. Its red Moorish castle affords wonderful views over orange groves and the fine red-tiled buildings of the town. Vikings, then a considerably long way from their Scandinavian home, once raided the town in AD 844. The attractive Gothic cathedral was built on top of the ruins of the earlier mosque once crusaders took the town in 1242. Some of the crusaders who perished are buried in the next-door Igreja da Misericórdia, which has a splendid example of a Manueline-style door. Down from the castle, towards the town centre, you pass through a number of imposing gates and past the impressive new Archaeology Museum, with its Moorish cistern, 10m (33ft) deep, left *in situ* in the middle of the floor.

Portimão, 9km (5 miles) west of Lagoa, is a modern, industrial city, but with a difference: this is one of the best

> **Fuel types for cars/trucks: unleaded (*sem-chumbo*), premium (*super*), diesel (*gasoleo*)**

places in Portugal to eat freshly grilled sardines at one of the many cheap waterside cafés. Portimão is also a good place to shop, though most of the goods on sale are imported and not locally produced. Worth a look is the central Largo 1° de Dezembro, where ten *azulejo* panels provide a lesson in Portuguese history across from the tourist office. Portimão's beach suburb is a short drive away, at **Praia da Rocha**, where you will find a beautiful 2km (1 mile) beach and all the attendant tourist facilities.

The Western Algarve

The intensity of tourist development noticeably diminishes as you head westwards from Portimão – though it is gradually creeping this way. **Lagos**, 17km (10 miles) west of Portimão, is one of the best bases in the Algarve (together with Tavira and Sagres). The quiet cobbled streets, enclosed by fine town walls, have survived the centuries, although many of the medieval buildings were lost to the 1755 earthquake. It was from here that Henry the Navigator, then Governor of the Algarve, launched his caravels on their mission to explore the world.

Highlights of the town are the golden splendour of the Igreja de Santo António, and the historical museums in the Forte da Ponte da Bandeira, as well as the Museu Regional de Lagos. Alongside the historical sights are countless small cafés and, for those in search of excitement, numerous busy nightclubs and bars.

The beaches are a short distance out of town. To the east lies the broad beach of **Meia Praia**. Far more scenic are the series of picture-perfect coves just to the south, including the popular **Praia de Dona Ana** and **Praia do Camilo**. More spectacular still is **Ponta da Piedade**, with stunning rock formations, cliffs and caves.

For a fine excursion inland, head for the scenic mountains of the **Serra de Monchique**, about 20km (12 miles) to the north of Portimão. The sound of running water pervades the lush countryside around the old spa town of **Caldas de Monchique**. In the 19th century this was a fashionable, genteel resort; now the old casino sells handicrafts, while water from the springs is bottled and sold all over the country.

This wide array of works on display testifies to the popularity of ceramics as an art form.

Monchique is the principal town in the area and is worth visiting to see the Manueline-style knotted stone ropes over the door of the Igreja Matriz. Above the town stands an old ruined convent, now occupied by goats, from where it is a short drive to the summit of **Foia** (902m/2,961ft). Despite a forest of antennae at the top, there are stunning

views of the south and west coasts and over the Serra de Monchique range.

The coast west from Lagos was, until recently, still relatively untouched, but villa and chalet settlements have sprung up at the small fishing villages of **Luz**, **Burgau** and **Salema**. The dramatic coastline carries on to the windswept cliffs of **Sagres**, famous as the base of Henry the Navigator's School of Navigation. Some claim his school was based at Lagos, but this lonely point, jutting out to sea at the extreme southwest tip of mainland Europe, seems far more appropriate as the setting for a daring school of Portuguese explorers.

The **Fortaleza** (Fortress) used by Henry dominates the coast from its clifftop promontory. Ironically, the number of visitors coming here in search of isolation has made it rather busy, and there is now even a pousada (see p.186). However, the wonderful beaches are not as crowded as in many other locations. For a greater sense of escape, head for the 'End of the Earth' (*Fim da Terra*), 6km (4 miles) away, at **Cabo São Vicente** (also known as the Sacred Promontory). Here you can enjoy an exhilarating walk that culminates in a view out to sea, over the steep cliffs, from the lighthouse.

North from Sagres, along the west coast, is the one part of the Algarve that may well escape intensive development, simply because, although the beaches are pleasant and the coastline dramatic, the water is colder and the wind stronger. For those interested in surfing or solitude, this coast may be ideal. **Aljezur**'s ruined Moorish castle looks over the town, which makes a good base for neighbouring beaches, such as the enormous rocky cove at **Arrifana** and the wider dune beach of **Monte Clerigo**, both of which also have their own small tourist complexes. Further north, **Odeceixe** is a pretty village set in a small river valley, which continues down to a wide cliff-backed beach at the estuary.

WHAT TO DO

SPORTS

The Algarve's gentle climate and excellent facilities make it by far the most popular region for sporting activities, but all sorts of sports can be enjoyed countrywide; ask the Portuguese National Tourist Office (see p.171) for a copy of its Sportugal brochure.

WATERSPORTS

Canoeing: there are plenty of opportunities, either in the sea or up a quiet river. Try exploring the River Guadiana from Alcoutim or Mértola.

These waters are a paradise for fishing.

Fishing: this is something of a national obsession, practised from both the shore and boats equipped for deep-sea fishing. Boats can be rented in Portimão, Faro, Sesimbra or Setúbal. A permit is needed for river and lake fishing; details are available from branches of the Portuguese National Tourist Office (see p.171), or Instituto Florestal, Avenida João Crisóstomo 26, 1000 Lisbon.

Jet-skiing, **sailing and water-skiing**: equipment can be hired at major resorts in the Algarve, on the Estoril Coast and on the Setúbal peninsula.

Scuba diving and snorkelling: over 30 centres round Portugal's long coastline cater for diving. It is especially popular in the western Algarve, at Luz, Lagos and Sagres, but is also catered for along the Estoril Coast and off Sesimbra.

Surfing: good surfing is available all along the wild western coast, particularly at Viana do Castelo, Ericeira, Guincho and the western Algarve.

Swimming: with great beaches all round the Portuguese coast, opportunities for swimming could not be better. The Algarve has warmer water and rather more sheltered beaches than the west coast, though many west coast resorts have sheltered bathing on their river estuaries. The water is very clean, except for some places near Oporto and Estoril. Lifeguards are not common. Most hotels have swimming pools.

Windsurfing: this is one of the most popular watersports in the Algarve, with a large number of sheltered spots providing somewhere to learn before striking out on the open sea. Tuition and rental is provided at most resorts. Good wave jumping conditions are found at the main surf locations (see above).

SPORTS ON LAND

Golf: Portugal has emerged as one of the world's top destinations for golfing holidays (ask the Portuguese National Tourist Office, see p.171, for their *Sportugal Golfing* brochure), with many companies offering all-inclusive holidays. There are top courses around Lisbon (especially Estoril) and a few around Oporto, but it is the Algarve which has the lion's share. Particularly notable are the three courses at Vilamoura and Quinta do Lago.

Hiking and mountain-biking: the main mountain ranges and national parks (see p.38) have waymarked paths. Enquire at local tourist offices for detailed information.

Horse-riding along the river – a marvellous way to take in this beautiful country.

Horse-riding: pony-trekking is one of the finest ways to explore the countryside, and there are stables all round the country where horses can be hired. Many *quintas* (hotels on country estates) provide horses for guests. Spectator sports include dressage at Queluz and Alter do Chão, and polo in Cascais. Although there is no regular horse-racing, you will find that there are occasional races in Estoril.

Hunting: this is popular with Portuguese during the season, which lasts from October to January. The main quarries are partridge, quail, hare, boar and deer. A large number of *quintas* (see above) offer hunting, notably in the Alentejo, Trás-os-Montes, Minho and mountainous parts of the Beiras. A licence is required from the Instituto Florestal (see Fishing on p.125), but this can often be arranged through your travel company. Vilamoura in the Algarve offers very good clay-pigeon shooting.

Skiing: there is a small-scale ski field operating in the Serra da Estrêla (see p.75).

Tennis: a large number of hotels and country houses have their own courts. The Algarve is home to several world-class tennis centres – one of the most impressive is at Vale do Lobo, where you can take a tennis holiday and be coached by former world-class players. The Estoril Tennis Club is another excellent centre.

SPECTATOR SPORTS

Bullfights: the dramatic Portuguese spectacle differs from the Spanish version, since the bull is not killed in the ring, but later in a slaughterhouse. The home of bullfighting is Vila Franca de Xira (see p.88) in the Ribatejo. Fights are also held in the Campo Pequeno in Lisbon, and may be organized for tourists along the Algarve coast during the bullfighting season – lasting from Easter Sunday to October.

Motor rallying: the Formula One Grand Prix rally is held in Estoril in late September.

Soccer: the national game stirs emotions, but without the violence that often accompanies football elsewhere. Football is a family game, and a good way to understand the Portuguese mind is to attend one of the matches. Top clubs include FC Porto, and Sporting and Benfica (both of Lisbon).

SHOPPING

Portugal's traditional arts and crafts, such as leatherwork or pottery, are justly famous and make reasonably priced souvenirs. These can be bought in *artesanatos* (craft shops), or direct from the artisans' workshops. Better still is to shop at one of Portugal's numerous fairs and markets (Barcelos, see p.34, is the biggest). The Chiado district, in Lisbon, is the most popular place to shop for international goods, while Loulé, in the Algarve, is one of the best places for crafts. The National Craft Fair in Vila do Conde, near Oporto (July and August), and the Craft Fair in Lagoa, in the Algarve (August), both display crafts from all over the country.

Shops are generally open from Monday to Friday, 9am to 1pm and 3pm to 7pm, and Saturday, from 9am to 1pm. Shopping centres stay open all day, often until late at night and on Sunday. Country markets start business around 8am and run through to mid-afternoon. Major credit cards are accepted in shops in the cities, but less so in the smaller towns. Prices are generally fixed, except in markets. Visitors who are not resident in the European Union can get sales tax refunds on large purchases (ask for details at the time of purchase).

A cheerful array of flowers in one of Lisbon's many bustling marketplaces.

WHAT TO BUY

Antiques: Lisbon is a major centre for antiques of all descriptions, from junk to high quality furniture and paintings. Rua Dom Pedro V, in the Bairro Alto, probably has the highest concentration of shops, though the Feira da Ladra in the Alfama is always worth a look (see p.95).

Azulejos: the traditional handpainted glazed tiles that

you come across have a very special place in the Portuguese heart. They range from historic blue and white to flamboyant and colourful modern designs. Good places to buy include the Azulejo Museum in Lisbon (see p.96) and the Azulejaria in Tomar (next door to the Museu dos Fosforos, Avenida Generale Bernardo Faria; tel. (049) 32 33 55), which will even make tiles to your own design.

Bedspreads: snug and warm embroidered *colchas* can be bought in Castelo Branco, in the Beira Baixa.

Brass, bronze and copper: the Moorish tradition of producing cooking utensils from beaten metal is still kept up in the town of Loulé, in the Algarve. The local wok-like pan, called a *cataplana*, makes a good buy.

Carpets: the centuries-old tradition of fine carpet-making survives in the Alentejo town of Arraiolos.

Clothing: Portugal is one of the world's leading producers of popular, inexpensive casual and sports clothing. For more traditional styles, try shopping around for chunky fishermen's sweaters or warm capes from the Alentejo.

Cork: as the world's leading producer of cork, Portugal offers all manner of cork items, ranging from ice buckets to sculptures, usually at very reasonable prices.

Embroidery: some of the world's finest hand embroidery comes from the islands of Madeira and the Azores, but also from mainland Portugal, particularly Viana do Castelo.

Filigree: gold and silver filigree jewellery, in styles dating from the Moorish occupation, is carefully fashioned in Gondomar, near Oporto.

Leather: stylish and inexpensive shoes, belts and bags are available all over Portugal, and count as one of the country's best buys.

Music: the haunting sound of *fado* (see opposite) makes an unusual and evocative memento. Also commonly available are cassettes featuring the lively sounds and rhythms of Portuguese/African bands.

Pottery: each region has its own distinctive style, ranging from the intricately painted faience animals of Coimbra, through the ubiquitous cockerel of Barcelos, to the black pottery of Chaves. All sorts of pots and mugs (and some very rude figures) make good, if fragile, presents.

Wickerwork: baskets, furniture and various other wickerwork items are sold in markets all over the country.

Wine: fine wines and fortified wines are an almost essential purchase – especially port and madeira (see p.141).

ENTERTAINMENT

Gambling: casinos are to be found at Monte Gordo, Vilamoura and Praia da Rocha (all in the Algarve), Estoril, Figuera da Foz, Espinho and Póvoa de Varzim. Popular games are baccarat, craps, roulette, black jack and slot machines. To be admitted, you must be over 21 and carry a passport.

Music: *fado* (see box below) is the most typically Portuguese of all music types, and its origins can be traced to the

---

Amália Rodrigues

Amália Rodrigues is fado's most famous star, the ultimate fadista (see above). She rose from a poor childhood in Lisbon to take the city by storm, a lone woman in a black dress singing in a characteristically intense style. She quickly conquered Portugal after her 1939 début and went on to thrill audiences in Madrid, Rio, Mexico City, New York and Paris, even spawning a new generation of Japanese fadistas.

Amália became a star of stage and screen, famous for her tempestuous love affairs. Recently she has also taken to singing poetry. Her music remains as popular as ever – one of her best albums is a collection of hits simply called O Fado.

---

wailing laments of Moorish and African slaves. The music survives in its purest form in Lisbon's Alfama district, *fado*'s spiritual home. Visits to the *fado* houses of the Alfama or Bairro Alto are a popular and unusual night out; the price is relatively high, but it does include supper. The *fadista*, usually a woman accompanied by two guitarists, belts out heart-wrenching songs of loss and misfortune, songs that are imbued with the kind of nostalgic yearning that the Portuguese call *saudade*. Coimbra also has its own more academic strand of *fado*, generally sung by male students.

Lisbon is home to most of the country's opera, ballet and classical concerts (the Gulbenkian Symphony is good), though there are some concerts in Oporto and tourist-oriented shows in the Algarve. Lisbon also enjoys a surfeit of jazz, rock and African music.

Nightlife: a number of bars, discos and clubs stay open virtually all night. The variety is endless, though they are mainly to be found in Lisbon and in the resorts of the Algarve. In smaller towns, things can be very quiet.

Theatre and cinema: theatre is also based in Lisbon and is almost exclusively performed in Portuguese. Films are invariably shown in their original language, together with Portuguese subtitles. For full details of screenings and performances, check the *Anglo-Portuguese News* (APN), the *Diário de Notícias* and the weekly *Se7e*.

FESTIVALS

Portugal has innumerable festivals, fairs, markets and the like. They take place all year round, but the peak season is around Easter and during the summer, especially around 15 August, the Feast of the Assumption. The north is famous for its religious processions, but there are plenty of non-religious festivals, too, celebrating all sorts of things, from

CALENDAR OF FESTIVALS AND EVENTS

A fuller list of events and information on precise dates can be obtained from the Portuguese Tourist Board (see p.171).

February-March: Carnival (Mardi Gras), with processions and fireworks all round the country.

March-April: Holy Week processions, including the famous one in Braga (Palm Sunday, Good Friday, Easter Sunday and Monday).

May *Barcelos*: Feast of the Crosses (first weekend). *Fátima*: Pilgrimage (up to the 13th). *Coimbra*: Queima das Fitas, the end of the University year (end of the month).

May-June: Algarve Music Festival in a number of towns.

June *Amarante*: Festival of São Gonçalo, attracts women seeking husbands (first weekend). *Lisbon*: Feasts of the People's Saints – Anthony (13th), John (24th), Peter (29th). *Santarém*: National Agricultural Fair, bullfights and festival (10 days from the first Friday).

July *Sintra*: Music Festival.

July-August *Vila do Conde*: National Handicrafts Fair.

August *Aveiro*: Festa da Ria, celebration of the lagoon lifestyle (last two weeks). *Viana do Castelo*: Festa da Nossa Senhora da Agonia, Viana's huge and famous *romaria*, or religious festival (weekend nearest to the 20th).

August-September *Lamego*: Pilgrimage to Nossa Senhora dos Remédios (last week in August to mid-September).

September *Palmela*: Wine Festival (middle of the month). *Ponte de Lima*: Feiras Novas, festival and markets (middle of the month). *Estoril*: Formula One Grand Prix (end of the month).

October *Fátima*: Pilgrimage (to the 13th). *Vila Franca de Xira*: Bull running, fair and bullfights (first Sunday). *Santarém*: National Gastronomic Fair (last 10 days).

November *Chaves*: Winter Fair (1st). *Golegã*: National Horse Show (first two weeks).

food to horses. Local saints' days also provide a good excuse for a party.

PORTUGAL FOR CHILDREN

The Portuguese adore children and make a great fuss over them. Aside from the cultural attractions of museums and castles, there are many playgrounds and you are likely to stumble across an itinerant fair or circus during your travels. Portugal dos Pequenitos, in Coimbra (see p.68), shrinks Portugal's most famous buildings down so that even kids tower over them. The narrow-gauge railways of the north also make a fun day-trip.

Of course the most popular destination for children is likely to be the beach. Most hotels also have pools, many with shallower pools for children alongside. The Algarve has a host of amusement parks, including waterslide parks such as Slide and Splash close by Lagoa and The Big One near Alcantarilha (there are similar parks near Lisbon and in the Alentejo). If performing dolphins and sealions appeal, then visit Zoo-Marine, near Albufeira. If your children want to mimic the exploits of Estoril's Formula 1 rally drivers, but at a slower pace, the Algarve has a number of parks with mini-racing cars.

Keeping the children happy need not be a balancing act – there's lots for them to enjoy.

EATING OUT

Portuguese cuisine is often described as the food of fishermen and farmers. You find the same dishes in the most
expensive places and in the simplest of cafés. The food is
generally good and cheap, made
with high-quality ingredients and
served in gargantuan portions (*uma
meia dose* is a half portion, usually
charged at two-thirds the price).
Seafood is excellent, as is much of
the meat, but vegetarians may have
a hard time. Portuguese cooks

> *Casas de fados*
> or *adegas típicas*
> are restaurants
> where you eat or
> drink to the
> sound of the *fado*.

favour herbs over spices, despite Moorish influence and Portugal's early involvement in the spice trade.

Some of the best dishes are regional stews, such as the *en-
sopadas* of the Alentejo, the *caldeiradas* of the Algarve and
the *açordas* of Estremadura. These dishes are often found in
restaurants all over the country. One of the characteristics of
Portuguese cooking is its daring combinations of ingredients, such as meat and seafood or fish and fruits. For a taste
of Portugal's great culinary variety, visit the National Gastronomic Fair in Santarém, in late October/early November.

WHERE AND WHEN TO EAT

Restaurants in Portugal are classified in four categories – *de
luxo* (luxury), *de primeira* (first-class), *de segunda* (second-
class) and *de terceira* (third-class). The price of a meal will
depend on the class, but of course the most expensive is not
always the best. *Típico* restaurants specialize in local cuisine,
marisqueirias in seafood and *churrasqueirias* in barbecues.

Often the *ementa turística* (tourist menu) offers good
value and a taste of the local cuisine. This is a set meal, usu-

ally consisting of bread, butter, soup, a main course, a dessert and a glass of wine. The *prato do dia* (dish of the day) is also inexpensive (even more so if you eat at the bar). When you sit down, remember that the tasty looking appetizers on your table will be charged for, unless you decide to have the *ementa turística*. Note also that shellfish is charged by the uncooked weight, so be careful how much you order. Tax and service is included in the bill, but a tip of between 5% and 10% should be left for good service.

Breakfast in Portugal (*o pequeno almoço*) is usually of the continental type, and lasts until around 10am (hotels will do cooked breakfasts on request and for an extra charge). Lunch (*o almoço*) is served from approximately 12.30pm until 3pm, and dinner (*o jantar*) from 7.30pm until 9.30pm or later.

WHAT TO EAT
Snacks

Snacks can be enjoyed almost everywhere, in a *salão de chá* (tea house), a *pastelaria* (pastry shop), a *tasca* (tavern), a *cervejaria* (beer house) or a snack bar. Some of the tastiest snacks are *rissóis* (meat patties), *lanches* (northern corn

A backdrop of azulejos in one of Portugal's numerous fine dining establishments.

bread stuffed with ham), *prego no pão* (steak sandwich), *pastéis* (flaked *bacalhau* – salt cod – in pastry) and *sandes mistas* (ham and cheese sandwich). The market is one of the best places to pick up snacks, and roast chestnuts (*castanhas*) are a great pick-me-up while exploring a city.

Soups and Starters

Açorda à Alentejana is an unusual soup of bread, coriander, egg and large amounts of garlic. *Caldo verde* (green soup) is one of Portugal's national dishes, a thick soup of shredded cabbage and potato, sometimes spiced up with a little *chouriço* sausage. *Sopa de pedra* (stone soup) is a marvellously thick country soup of numerous vegetables and meats. Adding the stone is optional. *Gaspacho* is familiar as the refreshing cold tomato and vegetable soup served in the south, but thicker than its Spanish cousin.

Portuguese bread is great and goes well with soup, especially *broa*, a corn bread from the north. Cold meats also go very well with bread, particularly *presunto* and *chouriço* (cured ham and sausage) from Trás-os-Montes and *espadarte fumado* (smoked sword fish) from Sesimbra.

Seafood and Fish

Fish plays an important part in the Portuguese diet and delicious fresh seafood is always available. Often you will see your soon-to-be dinner swimming in a tank at the front of a restaurant. Grilled *atum* (tuna) and *sardinhas* (sardines) are especially tasty.

Caldeirada de peixe is a sort of Algarvian bouillabaisse, a marvellous stew made from whatever small fish turn up in the fishermen's net. *Ameijoas na cataplana* is another stew from the Algarve, named after the wok-like pressure cooker (*cataplana*) in which it is usually cooked. Into this goes a

The Faithful Friend

Dried salt cod (bacalhau) is very close to the Portuguese heart and has been for centuries. Hot on the heels of Columbus (some say Portuguese fisherman got to America first), Portuguese cod fleets were fishing the Grand Banks off Newfoundland, salting and drying the cod on board the ship to create bacalhau. Overfishing has meant that Portugal now imports most of her bacalhau from Norway, Iceland and the Faroe Islands (where the largest fish factory is called the Bacalhau in honour of their main market).

Now that it is an imported dish, salt cod has gone from being a staple food to being an expensive delicacy. Even so, it is still immensely popular; it is said that there are 365 different ways to prepare it, one for each day of the year.

combination of clams (*ameijoas*), various meats, peppers, wine, garlic and onions.

Açorda de marisco is a bread-thickened shellfish soup into which raw eggs are folded just before it is served. *Truta com presunto* (trout with ham) consists of thinly sliced ham wrapped around river trout and then quickly sautéed in butter.

Perversely for a country so well supplied with fresh fish, salted cod (*bacalhau*) is the national dish (see box above). Salt cod is soaked overnight before serving and has a very strong flavour that takes some getting used to. Try it in baked dishes such as *bacalhau à Gomes de Sá* (flaked *bacalhau* with potatoes, onions and parsley, topped with olives and egg), or *bacalhau com natas* (with cream and potatoes).

Meat

Porco à Alentejana is the classic Portuguese meat dish, a mixture of marinated cubed pork cooked with small clams, paprika and garlic. Alternatively, try delicious *leitão assado* (suckling pig) especially if you happen to be in the small town of Mealhada, north of Coimbra.

Posta à Mirandesa is an enormous braised steak, as traditionally cooked in the Trás-os-Montes town of Miranda do Douro. *Feijoada à Transmontana* is a tasty stew of white beans mixed with various parts of a pig, plus ham, sausage and

Racks of Portugal's favourite fish, dried salt cod (bacalhau), for sale in Lisbon.

onions. Though not as elaborate as Brazilian *feijoadas*, this is still a stew to fill you up. Almost as daunting is *cozido*, a huge pile of boiled meats of all sorts, served with potatoes and cabbage; it's worth getting a friend to help you!

Liver (*fígado*) is a speciality of Lisbon, as is tripe (*tripas*) in Oporto. The meat stews (*ensopados*) of the Alentejo are not to be missed. All are likely to be served in large portions, with potatoes and rice. You should also note that the meat referred to as *vitela* (veal) is not the white veal of baby calves, but the red meat of young beef cattle.

Poultry and Game

Chicken (*frango*) is very popular and is often barbecued (*no churrasco*). *Frango piri-piri* is grilled in an African chilli sauce, while *frango na púcara* is cooked in a clay pot. Turkey (*peru*) is less common and is reserved for special occasions.

Portugal is a land of hunters, so many restaurants specialize in game (*caça*), particularly in the Alentejo, Trás-os-

Montes and Minho. During the season (autumn and winter), you can dine on venison (*veado*) and boar (*javali*); smaller game, such as rabbit (*coelho*), partridge (*perdiz*) and quail (*codorniz*) are common. A treat, if you can find it, is *perdiz estufada com castanhas* (partridge stuffed with chestnuts).

Non-meat Dishes

Vegetarianism has made few inroads in Portugal, and there are few vegetarian restaurants outside the capital and the Algarve. However, good fresh vegetables are often served as side dishes, including the popular broad beans (*favas*). Salads are readily available. A *salada à Portuguesa* is made with green peppers, garlic, tomato and cucumber. If you eat eggs, omelettes are served everywhere. Failing that, every town has a marketplace with all the ingredients to prepare your own wonderful dishes.

International Cuisine

Most restaurants stick exclusively to Portuguese cuisine, but, because of colonial connections, there are a fair number of Goan-style curry (*caril*) places, and Macau-style Chinese (Cantonese) restaurants. International chain hotels offer more familiar dishes and both Lisbon and the Algarve have various restaurants catering for tourists, but rarely as good or as inexpensive as their Portuguese equivalent.

Desserts and Cheese

The Portuguese are fond of sweets and the Moorish legacy has meant that sugar cakes, made with almonds, egg yolks and fruits, come in an endless variety. Originally made by the nuns of local convents, these cakes come with such names as 'bishop's tongues' (*línguas de bispo*) and 'nun's navels' (*barrigas de freira*).

Food and drink can be a very serious business – there's certainly no skimping.

Some of the most popular desserts are *pudim Molotov* (a light flan in caramel sauce), *arroz doce* (rice pudding), *ovos moles* (a paste of sugar, rice flour and egg yolks from Aveiro) and *queijada de Sintra* (Sintra cheesecake).

Cheeses using the milk of sheep and goats are very good, especially mountain cheese from the Serra da Estrêla in the Beiras (this area is demarcated, like a wine-producing region, to protect the quality and authenticity of the product). Serpa and Évora, both in the Alentejo, also produce excellent cheese. Look out, too, for *azeitão*, a small creamy cheese from a region to the south of the Tagus, and a yellow Edam-style cheese called *flamengo* (meaning 'Flemish').

DRINKS
Wine

A sign of the quality of Portuguese wines is that France is their largest importer. You can rarely go wrong with the house wine (*vinho da casa*); just tell the waiter whether you want *branco* (white) or *tinto* (red).

The alternative to red or white is 'green wine' (*vinho verde*). This fine young wine comes from the Minho and is made from both white and red grapes (white is better). The 'green' refers to the youth of the wine, or to the emerald colour of the Minho, depending on who you listen to. Other fine table wines come from the Dão region, near Viseu (mostly red), the Bairrada, south of Coimbra (both red and white), and from Lagoa in the Algarve. If you are looking for sparkle, try *vinho espumante*, a champagne-type wine.

> *À sua saude!* (ah sooer serooder)– cheers, literally "to your health"

Portugal is probably most famous for its fortified wines, port (see p.50) and madeira. Port wine comes in both traditional *digestif* varieties as well as lesser known dry white *apéritifs*. Madeira comes from the mid-Atlantic island of the same name and has long been popular all round the world.

Other Drinks

Portuguese lager-style beers, such as Sagres, are readily available all over the country. More local beers need seeking out, but you can sample them at the Silves Beer Festival (in the Algarve) in June.

Aguardente, distilled from grape skins and pips, is the local brandy. It is added to wine to make fortified port and madeira, and is delicious on its own, though certainly potent!

Portugal has many natural springs, so the bottled mineral water is excellent, especially Monchique, which is sold in still form (*sem gas*) and Luso, sold as still or fizzy (*com gas*). The usual soft drinks are available, but fresh fruit juice is surprisingly hard to find.

Tea and Coffee

Portugal, through her colonies, played a large part in introducing both tea and coffee to the world, and both drinks remain very popular. Coffee (*café*) is generally served as a strong black *bica* (like an expresso). *Carioca* is a diluted version, and a *garoto* is a *carioca* with a little milk, whereas *com leite* (or *galão*) is really milk with a dash of coffee.

Tea (*chá*) is served in a multitude of tea shops (*salão de chá*). These are not the result of any English influence – on the contrary, Catherine of Bragança introduced tea to the English court through her marriage to Charles II in 1662. Tea with milk is *chá com leite*; with lemon is *com limão*.

To Help You Order...

| Could we have a table? | **Queríamos uma mesa.** |
| Do you have a set-price menu? | **Tem uma ementa turística?** |

I'd like a ...		**Queria um/uma ...**	
beer	**cerveja**	mineral water	**água mineral**
bill	**conta**	napkin	**guardanapo**
bread	**pão**	omelette	**omelete**
butter	**manteiga**	pork	**porco**
chicken	**frango**	potatoes	**batatas**
coffee	**café**	salad	**salada**
dessert	**sobremesa**	sandwich	**sanduíche**
fish	**peixe**		**(sande)**
fruit	**fruta**	shellfish	**mariscos**
ice-cream	**gelado**	soup	**sopa**
lamb	**borrego**	sugar	**açúcar**
meat	**carne**	tea	**chá**
menu	**ementa**	vegetables	**legumes**
milk	**leite**	wine	**vinho**

...and Read the Menu

alho	garlic	frito	fried
almôndegas	meatballs	gambas	prawns
alperces	apricots	guisado	stew
ameijoas	baby clams	lagosta	spiny lobster
ananaz	pineapple	laranja	orange
arroz	rice	limão	lemon
assado	roast	linguado	sole
atum	tuna	lombo	fillet
bacalhau	codfish	lulas	squid
banana	banana	maçã	apple
batatas	potatoes	melancia	watermelon
besugo	sea bream	mexilhões	mussels
bife (vaca)	beef steak	molho	sauce
bolachas	biscuits	morangos	strawberries
bolo	cake	ostras	oysters
cabrito	kid	ovo	egg
camarão	shrimp	peixe	fish
caracóis	snails	pescada	hake
caranguejo	crab	pescadinha	whiting
cavala	mackerel	pêssego	peach
cebola	onion	pimento	green pepper
chouriço	spicy sausage	polvos	baby octopus
coelho	rabbit	presunto	ham
cogumelos	mushrooms	queijo	cheese
couve	cabbage	romãs	pomegranates
dobrada	tripe	salmonete	red mullet
dourada	sea-bass	salsichão	salami
enguias	eels	sardinhas	sardines
ervilhas	peas	torrada	toast
feijões	beans	truta	trout
flã	caramel	uvas	grapes
framboesas	raspberries	vitela	veal

INDEX

Where there is more than one set of references, the one in **bold** refers to the main entry. Page numbers in *italic* refer to an illustration.

BERLITZ TRAVEL TIPS

An A–Z Summary of Practical Information

> Listed after most main entries is an appropriate Portuguese
> translation, usually in the singular. You'll find this vocabulary
> useful when asking for information or assistance.

A

ACCOMMODATION (*alojamento*) (See also CAMPING on p.152,
YOUTH HOSTELS on p.176 and RECOMMENDED HOTELS on p.177)

Hotels in Portugal are graded from 5-star deluxe down to 2-star. The
other choices include an *estalagem* (an inn), a *pensão* (a room, often
with a meal included in the price), a *residencial* (a room, usually
without a meal), and self-catering apartments and villas, all of which
have their own 3-star down to 1-star system. Price limits are set for
every level in each category. Uncontrolled rooms (*quartos*) are also
offered in people's houses. These are of varying quality, so inspect
the room before agreeing to take it.

Pousadas are run by the government-owned ENATUR (Empresa
Nacional de Turismo). They are found all over the country, often in
beautiful and well-restored historic buildings, such as castles or convents, or in places of especial beauty. New pousadas opened in 1995
in Queluz and Crato. Tourist offices (see p.165) can give information
or you can contact ENATUR directly at Avenida Santa Joana Princesa 10, 1700 Lisbon, Portugal; tel. (01) 848 12 21/848 90 78/848 46
02, fax (01) 848 43 49/80 58 46. You can also book through
ENATUR agents in the UK: Keytel International, 402 Edgeware
Road, London W2 1ED; tel. (0171) 402-8182, fax (0171) 724-9503.

Portugal's **Turismo de Habitação** system, which started in the
Minho, has now spread all over the country and provides an intimate
view of rural life. In this system, people offer rooms in their privately
owned *quintas* (country houses), palaces and mansions. Breakfast is
always included and there are often sporting facilities. You can book
directly with the host or through one of the collective owners' organisations, the best known of which is Turihab, Praça da República,

4990 Ponte de Lima, Portugal; tel. (058) 74 16 72/74 28 27/74 28 29, fax (058) 74 14 44. The Portuguese National Tourist Office (see p.171) can also provide information on the various schemes.

Prices include tax and usually a continental breakfast. You will have to produce your passport when you check in.

I'd like a single/double room.	**Queria um quarto simples/duplo.**
with bath/shower	**com banho/chuveiro**
What is the rate per night?	**Qual é o preço por noite?**

AIRPORTS (*aeroporto*)

Portugal has three international airports: Lisbon, Faro and Oporto.

Lisbon airport is located in the northern suburb of Portela (the airport is sometimes also known by this name), about 15 minutes drive from the centre (allow longer in the rush hour). There are money-changing facilities, car-rental companies, a tourist office, a bar and restaurant, a duty-free shop and porters.

Frequent buses (44, 45 and Blue Bus 90) and many taxis offer transport to the city centre. Flight time information tel. (01) 80 20 60; general airport information tel. (01) 848 11 01.

Faro is the main base for charter flights to the Algarve. The airport is located just outside the town, towards the beach. Transport is provided by taxis, frequent buses (16), car-rental companies and the buses of tour operators. The airport has money-changing facilities, a tourist office (opening times erratic), a duty-free shop, bar, restaurant and post office. Airport information tel. (089) 81 82 81.

Oporto's Fransisco Sá Carneiro airport lies north of the town, towards Matasinhos. The facilities are similar to those at Faro. Bus 56 to the centre. For information tel. (02) 948 21 41.

Where do I get the bus to the airport/centre of the city?	**Onde posso apanhar o autocarro para o aeroporto/ o centro da cidade?**

B

BICYCLE RENTAL (*bicicletas de aluguer*)
Bicycles can be rented in many resorts and hotels. They can also be transported cheaply on the trains for longer journeys.

C

CAMPING (*campismo*)
There are dozens of sites all over the country. The Portuguese National Tourist Office (see p.171) can provide a list of all the sites, as can the Federaçao Portuguesa de Campismo, Rua Voz do Operário 1, 1000 Lisbon; tel. (01) 886 23 50.

You can only camp at recognized sites, and not on beaches or in forests. Some natural parks require camping permits and some sites require membership of an international camping organisation. You will also have to produce a passport.

Is there a campsite near here?	**Há algun parque de campismo por aqui perto?**
May we camp here?	**Podemos acampar aqui?**
We have a caravan (trailer).	**Temos uma roulotte.**

CAR RENTAL (*carros de aluguer*) (See also DRIVING on p.157 and PLANNING YOUR BUDGET on p.165)
International and locally owned companies flourish in the cities and at the airports. A recommended company is Auto Cerro, based in the Algarve, at Estrada dos Caliços, Apartado 2063, 8200 Albufeira; tel. (089) 58 64 25/6/7, fax (089) 58 64 28/9. They have offices throughout the Algarve and in Lisbon and Oporto. Cars can often be hired at a better rate through booking in advance by means of a fly-drive package.

You must be 21 to rent a car (25 for some companies) and have held a licence for at least a year. A deposit or credit-card voucher is required. Third party insurance is included, and collision and personal accident waivers are an option. Using the car to travel to Spain will usually incur an additional insurance charge.

I'd like to hire a car today/tomorrow.	**Queria alugar um carro para hoje/amanhã.**
for one day/a weekend/a week	**por um dia/o fim da semana/uma semana**
which includes full insurance	**que inclua um seguro contra todos os riscos, por favor**

CLIMATE and CLOTHING (*clima; roupa*)

Portugal's climate is kind, especially in the exceptionally sunny Algarve. Summers are warm and winters mild. Further north the weather can be cold in winter, especially in the interior mountains.

The following chart shows the average air and sea temperatures:

	Jan	Mar	May	July	Sept	Nov
Lisbon						
Air temp. °C/°F	11/52	14/57	17/63	22/72	22/72	14/57
Sea temp. °C/°F	15/59	17/63	19/66	21/70	19/66	16/61
Faro						
Air temp. °C/°F	12/54	13/55	18/65	24/75	22/72	16/61
Sea temp. °C/°F	15/59	17/63	19/66	21/70	19/66	16/61
Bragança						
Air temp. °C/°F	4/39	8/47	13/55	21/70	17/63	8/46

Clothing (*roupa*). The Algarve has a Mediterranean climate and you may find a sweater will be needed for some evenings. Further north, warmer clothes should be brought, especially if you are going inland or to mountainous regions. Most restaurants are informal, but you may want to bring a jacket and tie for grander establishments.

Will I need a tie?	**É preciso gravata?**
Is it all right if I wear this?	**Vou bem assim?**

Portugal

COMMUNICATIONS (See also TIME DIFFERENCES on p.170)

Post offices (*correios*). The mail service is fairly good. Mailboxes are British-style pillar boxes, red for normal post and blue for the slightly faster (and more expensive) *Correio Azul* (which simply means 'Blue Post') service. Post offices are open Monday-Friday, 9am-7pm, and major city-centre offices are open on Saturday until noon as well (Lisbon airport has a 24-hour service). Local shops also sell stamps (*sellos*).

You can use main post offices for *poste restante* facilities. Simply have your mail addressed Posta Restante, followed by the postal code and town name (for example, Mr J Smith, Posta Restante, 8200 Albufeira, Portugal). To make things easier, underline surnames on the envelope. You will need to show a passport and pay a small fee to pick up your letters.

Have you received any mail for...?	**Tem correio para...?**
A stamp for this letter/postcard, please.	**Um selo para esta carta/este postal, por favor.**
express (special delivery)	**expresso**
airmail	**via aérea**
registered	**registado**
poste restante	**posta restante**

Telephones (*telefone*) **and fax**. Phone booths take 10, 20 and 50 escudos coins; unused ones are returned. Card phones (*Credifone*) use prepaid cards available from shops displaying the Credifone sign, and from post offices. Often the easiest way is to call from a post office or phone centre and then pay at the counter.

International Direct Dialling is now the norm, even from street booths. Dial 00 to make an international call, then the country code (44 for the UK, 1 for the US), followed by the area code (leaving off the initial zero) and the number. Dial 099 for the European operator, 098 for the rest of the world.

To call from overseas, dial the international access code (00 in the UK, 011 in the US), then Portugal's country code (351), followed by the area code (leaving off the initial zero) and the number.

Telephone numbers regularly change in Portugal, and for no apparent reason. Make sure you use an up-to-date phone book.

You can send faxes from post offices or hotels. In Lisbon, Marconi Company, Rua São Julião 131, runs a 24-hour international service.

reverse-charge (collect) call	**paga pelo destinatário**
Can you get me this number in...?	**Pode ligar-me para este número em...?**
May I send a fax to...?	**Quero mandar um fax para...?**

COMPLAINTS (*reclamação*)

Complaints should be sorted out on the spot if possible. If not, ask for the *livro de reclamações* (complaints book), which all hotels, restaurants and tourist companies are obliged to keep. Make sure you retain a copy of your entry. You can also try writing to the manager of the establishment, the local tourist office or the head office of the Department of Tourism, Avenida António Augusto de Aguiar 86, 1100 Lisbon; tel. (01) 57 52 86. Keep all documents and copies of correspondence to show your travel agent or insurance company.

CRIME (*delito*) (See also EMERGENCIES on p.160 and POLICE on p.168)

Although Portugal is a safe country, it is always worth being careful, especially in cities where pick-pockets and bag snatchers operate. Leave valuables in a hotel safe and don't leave them unattended on the beach while swimming. Theft from parked cars (especially rental cars) is very common. Leave nothing of value in them, as this sort of crime has rocketed in recent years, not only in the Algarve but all over Portugal. Violent crime is rare, but the cities do have a growing drugs problem.

Portugal

Report any crime to the police (who will make a small charge for taking your statement, but obtaining this is necessary for later insurance claims), as well as to your hotel or tour representative.

I want to report a theft.   **Quero participar um roubo.**

CUSTOMS (*alfândega*) and ENTRY FORMALITIES
Visitors from northern America, the European Union and the Commonwealth need only a valid passport to visit Portugal for 90 days (60 for US citizens). The Portuguese-Spanish border scarcely serves as a frontier anymore, and visitors can come and go with ease.

Currency restrictions. Sums in excess of 1 million escudos in value must be declared on entry, and you cannot take out of the country more foreign currency than you brought in. You may not export more than 100,000 escudos in local currency, per person per trip.

Customs. There is no limit on the amount of goods that can be brought into Portugal from another EU member country, but strict limits apply to the amount of duty-free goods that can be imported from outside the EU. The allowances are as follows: 200 cigarettes or 50 cigars or 250g of tobacco; 1 litre of spirits (liquor), or 2 litres of liqueurs or fortified wines below 22% alcohol, or 2 litres of sparkling wine; and 2 litres of table wine.

Allowances for non-EU residents returning home are: **Australia**: 200 cigarettes or 250g of tobacco or cigars; 1 litre of spirits or wine; **Canada**: 200 cigarettes and 50 cigars and 900g of tobacco; 1.1 litre of spirits or wine or 8.5 litres of beer; **New Zealand**: 200 cigarettes or 50 cigars or 250g of tobacco; 4.5 litres of wine or beer and 1.1 litre of spirits; **South Africa**: 400 cigarettes and 50 cigars and 250g of tobacco; 2 litres of wine and 1 litre of spirits; **USA**: 200 cigarettes and 100 cigars or a 'reasonable amount' of tobacco, plus 1 litre of spirits and 1 litre of wine.

I have nothing to declare.   **Não tenho nada a declarar.**
It's for my personal use.   **É para uso pessoal.**

D

DRIVING IN PORTUGAL (See also Car Rental on p.152 and
Emergencies on p.160)
If you are driving your own car, you will need your national driving
licence, registration documents and at least third party insurance
(comprehensive insurance is recommended). Carry all these documents with you when driving. A warning triangle must be used in the
event of an accident or breakdown. Seat belts must be worn.

Driving conditions. Drive on the right and overtake on the left. Cars
already on a roundabout have right-of-way unless otherwise indicat-
ed by road markings or lights. Portugal has the highest accident rate
in Europe, so caution is essential. Drivers flash their lights to mean
that they are coming through, rather than that you should go on. In
theory, pedestrians have right-of-way, but do not count on this.

Speed limits. 120kph (75mph) on motorways, 90kph (56mph) on
other roads and 60kph (37mph) in built-up areas. Minimum speeds
are posted in blue. Cars towing caravans may not exceed 50kph
(30mph) in towns and 70kph (45mph) on open roads. Motorways
and major bridges usually have tolls.

Parking. You must park in the direction of the traffic flow. Normally
you can park as long as you wish, except in a 'Blue Zone', where you
have to buy a ticket from a machine. Leave sidelights on in dark
places. In Lisbon it is often best to use car parks.

Repairs. Members of motoring organisations affiliated to the *Au-
tomóvel Clube de Portugal* (Rua Rosa Araújo 24, Lisbon; tel. (01)-
356 39 31) can use their repair and emergency facilities for free.
Otherwise garages can fix most things. On the larger roads you will
find SOS telephones.

Road signs. Standard international signs are used in Portugal. Here
are some of the signs you are likely to see:

Alto	Halt
Cruzamento	Crossroads

Portugal

Curva perigrosa	Dangerous bend
Descida ingreme	Steep hill
Desvio	Diversion
Encruzilhada	Crossroads
Estacionamento permitido	Parking allowed
Estacionamento pro'bido	No parking
Guiar com cuidado	Drive with care
Obras/Fim de obras	Roadworks/end of roadworks
Paragem de autocarro	Bus stop
Pare	Stop
Passagem proibida	No entry
Pedestres, peões	Pedestrians
Perigo	Danger
Posto de socorros	First-aid post
Pro'bida a entrada	No entry
Saída de camiões	Lorry/truck exit
Seguir pela direita/esquerda	Keep right/left
Sem saída	No through road
Sentido proibido	No entry
Sentido único	One-way street
Silêncio	Silence (no horns or excessive noise)
Trabalhos	Roadworks
Trânsito proibido	No through traffic
Veículos pesados	Heavy vehicles
Velocidade máxima	Maximum speed

Are we on the right road for...? **É esta estrada para...?**

Fill the tank with super, please.	**Encha o depósito de super, por favor.**
Check the oil/tyres/ battery, please.	**Verifique o óleo/os pneus/ a bateria, se faz favor.**
I've broken down.	**O meu carro está avariado.**
There's been an accident.	**Houve um accidente.**

Fluid measures

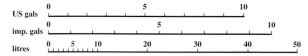

Distance

ELECTRIC CURRENT (*corrente eléctrica*)
The standard supply is 220-230volts, 50Hz, with round continental-style two-pin plugs. Hotels usually have a 110-volt shaver outlet. US equipment will need both a plug adaptor and a voltage transformer.

I need an adaptor/ a battery, please.	**Preciso de um adaptador/ uma pilha, por favor.**

EMBASSIES and CONSULATES (*embaixada; consulado*)
Embassies are listed in local phone books (under *Consulado* or *Embaixada*). Most are in Lisbon, Oporto, or Faro.

Australia (Embassy): Avenida da Liberdade 244, 4º, Lisbon; tel. (01) 52 33 50.

Canada (Embassy): Avenida da Liberdade 144, 3º, Lisbon; tel. (01) 347 48 92; (Consulate): 1.1º E Fr Lourç Santa Maria, Faro; tel. (089) 80 37 57.

Portugal

Republic of Ireland (Embassy): Rua da Impresa a Estrêla 1, 4°, Lisbon; tel. (01) 396 15 69.

Japan (Embassy): Rua Mouzinho da Silveira 11, Lisbon; tel. (01) 352 34 85.

South Africa (Embassy): Avenida Luis Bivar 10/10 A, Lisbon; tel. (01) 53 50 41.

United Kingdom (Embassy): Rua São Domingo à Lapa 37, Lisbon; tel. (01) 396 11 91; (Consulate): Rua da Estrêla 4, 1200 Lisbon; tel. (01) 395 40 83; (Consulate): Avenida Boavista 3072, Oporto; tel. (02) 618 47 89; (Consulate): 7.1° Largo Fransisco A Maurício, Portimão; tel. (082) 41 78 00.

United States (Embassy): Avenida Forças Armadas 16, Lisbon; tel. (01) 726 66 00.

Most embassies and consulates are open from Monday to Friday, 9am or 10am-5pm, with a one to two-hour lunch break.

Where is the British/American embassy?	**Onde é a embaixada inglesa/americana?**
It is very urgent.	**É muito urgente.**

EMERGENCIES (*urgência*) (See also MEDICAL CARE on p.164 and DRIVING IN PORTUGAL on p.157)
The following free numbers are available 24 hours a day for emergencies:

Police and general emergency	**115**
Fire	**342 22 22, 60 60 60**
Ambulance (Red Cross)	**301 77 77**

Blue phone boxes on the street go straight through to the police, but generally the person who answers will only speak Portuguese.

ETIQUETTE

The Portuguese will probably address you as *senhor* or *senhora*. Even so, people are very hospitable. Shake hands on meeting and parting. To attract your attention, someone may tap you on the arm.

The Portuguese wear casual clothes but are rarely sloppy. Nude and topless swimming is taken for granted in the Algarve, but it still makes many Portuguese uncomfortable. It is best to see what everyone else is doing before whipping off your clothes.

GAY and LESBIAN TRAVELLERS
Portugal is a devoutly religious country and gay life is not as open as in some parts of Europe, though there are no specific laws against homosexuality (the age of consent is 16). There are gay bars and clubs in Lisbon, such as Trumps, Rua da Imprensa Nacional 104b, and Memorial, Rua Gustavo de Matos Sequeira 42a. Beach number 9, on the Costa da Caparica, is gay. There are also gay clubs and beaches in Oporto and the Algarve. For more details, contact Gay International Rights, PO Box 110, 4702 Braga Codex, Portugal; tel. (053) 792 96.

GUIDES and TOURS
All guides must be a member of the Portuguese professional guides' association. English-speaking guides can be arranged through local tourist offices or travel agents, or in Lisbon at Rua do Telhal 4, 3°; tel. (01) 346 71 70 (open 9am-1pm and 2.30pm-6pm).

Bus, boat and walking tours can also be arranged through tourist offices and travel agents.

We would like an English-speaking guide/interpreter.

Queremos um guia que fale inglês/um intérprete de inglês.

LANGUAGE
Portuguese is the world's seventh most spoken language. A knowledge of Italian, French or Spanish will help you understand written Portuguese, though the unique pronunciation may be harder to crack. French is commonly spoken as the second language in Portugal, par-

ticularly amongst returned emigrants in the north. English is often known in tourist areas, but not much outside.

The Berlitz PORTUGUESE PHRASE BOOK AND DICTIONARY covers practically all the situations you are likely to encounter on your travels, and includes the optional extra of a cassette or CD to help you practice your new phrases. Also useful is the Berlitz PORTUGUESE-ENGLISH/ENGLISH-PORTUGUESE DICTIONARY, which has a grammar section and menu-reader supplement.

On the cover of this guide you'll find a list of useful expressions. Here are a number of other commonly used words and phrases:

Good evening	**Boa noite**
Goodbye	**Adeus**
excuse me/you're welcome	**perdão/de nada**
where/when/how	**onde/quando/como**
yesterday/today/tomorrow	**ontem/hoje/amanhã**
day/week/month/year	**dia/semana/mês/ano**
left/right	**esquerdo/direito**
good/bad	**bom/mau**
big/small	**grande/pequeno**
cheap/expensive	**barato/caro**
hot/cold	**quente/frio**
old/new	**velho/novo**
open/closed	**aberto/fechado**
Please write it down.	**Escreva-mo, por favor.**
What does it mean?	**Que quer dizer isto?**
Help me, please.	**Ajude-me, por favor.**
Just a minute.	**Um momento.**
Get a doctor quickly.	**Chame um médico, depressa.**
What day is it today?	**Que dia é hoje?**

DAYS

Sunday	**domingo**	Thursday	**quinta-feira**
Monday	**segunda-feira**	Friday	**sexta-feira**
Tuesday	**terça-feira**	Saturday	**sábado**
Wednesday	**quarta-feira**		

LAUNDRY and DRY CLEANING (*lavandaria; tinturaria*)

Bigger hotels offer this service, though not cheaply. Self-service launderettes can be found in cities (look under *Lavandarias e Tinturarias* in the *Yellow Pages*). They are usually open 9am-1pm, 3pm-7pm on weekdays and from 9am to noon on Saturday.

Dry cleaning usually takes three or four days, though some offer a next-day service.

When will it be ready?	**Quando estará pronto?**
I must have this for tomorrow morning.	**Preciso disto para amanhã de manhã.**

LOST PROPERTY (*objectos perdidos*)

Having checked with your hotel or the public transport authorities, report your loss to the local police station and get confirmation that you have done so for your insurance claim.

There is no central lost property office in the Algarve, but in Lisbon the police have a lost property number: tel. (01) 346 61 41. If you lose something on Lisbon public transport, go to the lost-and-found office at the base of the Santa Justa lift, near the Rossio, or tel. (01) 347 08 77.

I have lost my wallet/purse/passport.	**Perdi a minha carteira/mala/passaporte.**

M

MEDIA

Radio and Television (*rádio; televisão*). There are four TV channels, two government-run and two independent. Films are usually shown in their original language but imported TV programmes are dubbed. Spanish channels can also be picked up. Larger hotels offer satellite and cable channels in English, Spanish, German and Italian.

There are four government radio stations. Programme Two broadcasts classical music while Programme Four is for pop. Travel suggestions are broadcast in English on Programme Two (755 kHz medium wave, 94.3 Mhz FM) at 8.15am. English-language stations, such as the BBC World Service, Voice of America and Radio Canada International, can be picked up at different times of the day.

Newspapers and Magazines (*jornal; revista*). Several English-language newspapers are published locally, including the *Anglo-Portuguese News* (APN). International newspapers and magazines are widely available. In Lisbon, check *Diário de Noticias* and *Se7e* for cinema and theatre listings; other towns have their own versions.

Have you any English-language **Tem jornais em inglês?**
newspapers?

MEDICAL CARE (See also EMERGENCIES on p.160)
Tourist offices often hold lists of English-speaking doctors. In Lisbon, you can contact the British Hospital (tel. (01) 60 20 20), for advice, but they do not have a casualty department.

Make sure your travel insurance has a good medical plan. Residents of European Union countries can get free emergency treatment in Portugal. Bring along the E111 social security form (available from post offices at home) and show it to the doctor in Portugal, making clear you are an EU resident. Without this you will be charged for medical and dental treatment and medicines, but keep all receipts and documents if you wish to make an insurance claim.

Chemists (*Farmácias*). Pharmacies are open normal business hours. A notice will be posted in the window with details of the pharmacy open 24 hours; details are also published in local newspapers.

Where is the nearest (all night) **Onde fica a farmácia**
pharmacy? **(de serviço) mais proxima?**

a doctor	**um médico**
a dentist	**um dentista**
an ambulance	**uma ambulância**
hospital	**hospital**
an upset stomach	**mal de estômago**
sunstroke	**uma insolação**
a fever	**febre**

MONEY MATTERS (See also CUSTOMS AND ENTRY FORMALITIES on p.156)

Currency (*moeda*). The escudo ('shield', abbreviated as esc or PTE) is represented as a $ replacing the decimal point, so 2,000$00 means 2,000 escudos and 0 centavos (the latter are rarely used these days). Coins come in 1, 2½, 5, 10, 20, 50, 100 and 200 escudo denominations, and notes in 500, 1,000 (equal to one conto), 5,000 and 10,000.

Exchange facilities (*câmbio*). Normal banking hours are Monday-Friday, 8.30am-2.30pm or 2.45pm, with some banks closing for lunch 11.45am-1pm In tourist areas and at airports, banks often remain open later.

You can change money at banks and exchange houses, with varying rates and commissions. Hotels often change money, but at a high price. In tourist areas, many banks have hole-in-the-wall machines for changing foreign currency notes to escudos.

| May I change some pounds/ dollars, please. | **Queria trocar libras/dólares, por favor.** |

Credit cards (*cartão de crédito*). Credit cards are accepted in tourist establishments and at petrol stations (with a 100 escudos surcharge). ATM machines can be used for drawing money on credit cards. To report a lost or stolen card, call UNICRE; tel. (01) 53 35 60 or your own card issuer's emergency telephone number.

Portugal

Can I pay with this credit card?	**Posso pagar com cartão de crédito?**

Travellers' cheques (*cheque de viagem*). Travellers' cheques usually attract a fairly hefty charge when you change them, and you will need to show your passport. Some tourist shops will accept them. Eurocheques are widely accepted.

Can you cash a travellers' cheque?	**Pode pagar um cheque de viagem?**

Planning your budget

The following list will give you a rough idea of prices in Portugal.

Airport transfer. 150 esc on the bus (in Lisbon the special airport bus is 400 esc). Taxi to centre of town about 2,000 esc.

Bicycle hire. 1,000-2,000 esc per day.

Car rental (local company). *Renault Twingo* (2 door) 4,300 esc per day unlimited mileage. *Ford Orion* (4 door) 11,500 esc per day unlimited mileage. Add 16% tax. Lower rates can be arranged if booked in advance from abroad or for weekends. International companies are more expensive.

Entertainment. Bullfight from 2,000 esc; cinema 400 esc; disco from 1,000 esc; *fado* from 5,000 esc; casino entrance 1,000 esc.

Food and drink. Prices are per person. Continental breakfast from 500 esc; lunch and dinner (excluding drink) in a good establishment from 2,500 esc; coffee from 50 esc, beer from 100 esc, Portuguese brandy from 100 esc, gin and tonic from 400 esc, bottle of house wine from 600 esc.

Guides. 9,000-12,000 esc per half day, 16,000-20,000 esc per day.

Hotels (double room with bath per night). 5-star 42,000 esc and up; 4-star 28,000 esc; 3-star 15,000 esc; 2-star 9,200 esc; 1-star 5,000 esc. Pension 4,000-6,000 esc.

Petrol. 150 esc per litre.

Public transport. Metro 60 esc from machine, 70 esc from ticket office, 10 tickets for 500 esc; bus and tram 150 esc, or 20 tickets for 700 esc. Tourist pass for four days on Lisbon's public transport system 1,600 esc, 7 days 2,000 esc.

Sports. Golf 6,000-12,500 esc for green fees for 18-hole championship course. Club and trolley hire around 3,500 esc. Horse-riding 2,500-3,500 esc per hour. Tennis 1,000 esc per court per hour. Equipment hire: racquets 400 esc, balls 300 esc. Water-skiing 5,000 esc per session. Jet-skiing 2,000 esc per 10 minutes. Tuition for most sports 5,000-6,000 esc per hour.

Taxi. Initial charge of 200-250 esc, then 60-70 esc per km. Higher rates at night and for luggage.

OPENING HOURS (*horas de abertura*)

Banks: 8.30am-2.30pm or 2.45pm; some have a lunch break from 11.45am to 1pm.

Bars and restaurants. In tourist areas, from noon to the early hours of the morning. More upmarket restaurants will only open at meal times. Many restaurants close one day a week.

Markets. 8am-1pm.

Museums. Usually open Tuesday to Sunday, 10am-5pm (some open until 6pm or 6.30pm in summer). Most close for lunch from 12.30pm or 1pm until 2pm or 2.30pm.

Offices. Monday-Friday, 9am to 1pm and 3pm to 7pm.

Post offices. Main offices, Monday-Friday, 8.30am or 9am-6.30pm or 7pm, and Saturday, 8.30am to noon. Local branches, Monday-Friday, 9am-12.30pm and 2pm-6pm.

Shops. Monday-Friday, 9am-1pm and 3pm-7pm, Saturday 9am-1pm. Large shopping centres stay open later and may be open during lunch and on Sundays.

P

PHOTOGRAPHY (*fotografia*) (See also VIDEO on p.175)

International brands of film are easy to find in all locations. Colour processing takes two or three days, though there are plenty of city centre and tourist outlets offering a one-hour service. It is best to bring transparencies (slides) home for processing.

Do not take photographs of airports or military bases.

For handy tips on how to get the most out of your holiday photographs, purchase a copy of the Berlitz-Nikon GUIDE TO TRAVEL PHOTOGRAPHY (available in the UK only).

I'd like some film for this camera.	**Quero um rolo para esta máquina.**
a black-and-white film	**um rolo a preto e branco**
a colour film	**um rolo a cores**
a colour-slide film	**um rolo de diapositivos a cores**
35mm film	**um rolo de trinta e cinco milímetros**
How long will it take to develop this film?	**Quanto tempo leva a revelar este filme?**
May I take a picture?	**Posso tirar uma fotografia?**

POLICE (*polícia*) (See also EMERGENCIES on p.160)

The state police (PSP) deal with routine police matters and traffic control in towns. Few speak English, but they do their best to be helpful. In tourist areas, look for police with armbands reading CD (*Corpo Disitral*); they are there to help tourists and they all speak at least one other language than Portuguese. The GNR (*Guarda Nacional Republicana*) deals with serious crime, and they also patrol the national highways. The correct way to address a policeman is 'Senhor Guarda'.

Where is the nearest police
station?

**Onde fica o posto de polícia
mais próximo?**

PUBLIC HOLIDAYS (*feriado*)

1 January	*Ano Novo*	New Year's Day
February	*Carnaval*	Shrove Tuesday/ Mardi Gras
March/April	*Sexta-feira Santa*	Good Friday
25 April	*Dia da Liberdade*	Liberty Day
1 May	*Festa do Trabalho*	Labour Day
May/June	*Corpo de Deus*	Corpus Christi
10 June	*Dia de Camões*	Camões' Day
15 August	*Assunção*	Assumption
5 October	*Heróis da República*	Republic Day
1 November	*Todos-os-Santos*	All Saints' Day
1 December	*Dia da Independência*	Independence Day
8 December	*Imaculada Conceição*	Immaculate Conception
25 December	*Natal*	Christmas

Other than these national holidays, every community has a number
of local holidays, usually commemorating local saints.

Are you open tomorrow?

Estão abertos amanhã?

R

RELIGION

The overwhelming number of Portuguese are Roman Catholic.

In Lisbon, English-speaking Catholics can attend Sunday mass at
the Dominican Church of Corpo Santo, Travessa do Corpo Santo 32.
Anglican services are held on Sundays at St George's Church, in the
Estrêla district of Lisbon, and at St Paul's, Avenida Bombeiros Vol-

untarios 1c, Estoril. Church of Scotland (Presbyterian) services are held on the first Sunday of every month at Rua da Arriaga 11; tel. (01) 66 30 10. The Shaare Tikva Synagogue is at Rua Alexandre Herculano 59; tel. (01) 65 86 04. For other places, denominations or religions, ask your hotel concierge, or at the local tourist office.

T

TIME DIFFERENCES
Portugal observes the same time as Spain and France, that is GMT plus one hour from the last Sunday in September until the last Sunday in March, and GMT plus two hours for the rest of the year. Thus, in **summer**, the time differences are as follows:

New York	London	Paris	**Lisbon**	Jo'burg	Sydney	Auckland
6am	11am	noon	**noon**	noon	8pm	10pm

What time is it, please?   **Que horas são, por favor?**

TIPPING
Hotel and restaurant bills usually include service, but often an extra tip is expected.

Hairdresser/barber	10%
Hotel maid, per week	500 esc
Lavatory attendant	25-50 esc
Hotel Porter, per bag	100 esc
Taxi driver	10%
Tour Guide	10% to 15% of excursion fare
Waiter	5% to 10% of the bill

TOILETS (*lavabo/sanitario/toilete/retrete/casa de banho*)
Don't expect any paper at public toliets. You can always use the facilities in larger hotels, cafés or bars, so long as you buy a drink. Toilets for men are marked *Homens*; those for women, *Senhoras*.

Where are the toilets please?   **Onde são as casas de banho, por favor?**

TOURIST OFFICES (*Turismo*)

Canada: Portuguese National Tourist Office, Suite 1005, 60 Bloor Street West, Toronto, Ontario M4W 3B8; tel. (416) 921 7376.

Japan: Portuguese National Tourist Office, Regency Shinsaka 101, 8-5-8 Akasaka, Minato-ku, Tokyo; tel. (03) 5474 4400.

United Kingdom: Portuguese National Tourist Office, 2nd Floor, 22/25a Sackville Street, London W1X 1DE; tel. (0171) 494 1441.

United States: Portuguese National Tourist Office, 590 Fifth Avenue, New York, NY 10036; tel. (212) 354 4403.

In **Lisbon**, the National Tourist Office is at Avenida António Augusto de Aguiar 86; tel. (01) 315 50 91. The most central is the information office in Palácio Foz, on the Praça dos Restauradores; tel. (01) 346 36 43. English-language tourist information can be obtained by phone; tel. (01) 70 63 41.

Virtually every town has a local tourist office (*Turismo*).

TRANSPORT

Public transport generally runs from around 6am or 7am to midnight or 1am.

Local buses (*autocarros*) and **trams** (*eléctricos*). Bus and tram stops in cities usually have a small route map and an indication of which buses stop there. You can buy your ticket on the bus, or you can buy passes or blocks of tickets from kiosks and some shops (if in doubt, ask at the tourist office).

Underground (*Metro*). Lisbon has two lines. This offers a fast way of getting around, though there is a limited number of stops.

Taxis. Most taxis are black with a green roof and a 'taxi' sign; in the country, any car marked with an 'A' (meaning *aluguer*, 'for hire') is a taxi. City taxis have meters, but are entitled to charge an extra 20% at night and an extra sum for each item of luggage. Tip about 10%. If there is no meter, it is essential to establish a price before your journey starts. Most taxis use taxi stands, but some cruise the streets looking for passengers.

Intercity buses. Intercity buses are a fairly fast, comfortable and a cheap way of getting around Portugal. The majority of buses are operated by RN (Rodoviária Nacional), except in the Minho and Trás-os-Montes areas, where there is a profusion of different companies. Buses are likely to operate out of the same central bus station, though in cities there can be several stations, in which case it is worth asking for advice at the tourist office. The bus network is far more extensive than the train system.

Trains (*comboio*). Trains are operated by CP (Caminhos de Ferro Portugueses), the national rail company. Many lines have closed in recent years, to be replaced by buses. Regional trains stop at most stations, intercity trains cost more and make fewer stops, while express (*Rápido*) trains run from Lisbon to Oporto non-stop and cost still more. Direct services from Oporto and Lisbon to the Algarve are available on the *Comboio Azul* (the 'Blue Train').

All trains have first and second-class carriages. Tickets cost less on 'Blue Days' (*Dias Azuis*), which usually occur in the middle of the week. Discounts of 50% are available for senior citizens (though you first need to get a free Cartão Dourada) on trains running from 6.30am to 9.30am, and from 5pm to 8pm, except at weekends and on public holidays, and on suburban trains. As a rule, prices are lower than in most western European countries. *Bilhete Turisticos* offer unlimited train travel for 7, 14 or 21 days. Inter-rail, Inter-rail 26 plus, Rail Europe Senior and Eurail passes are all valid in Portugal.

Lisbon is the central hub of the train network. There are four stations: Santa Apolónia for international services and to northern Portugal; Cais do Sodré for commuter trains to the western suburbs, and to Estoril and Cascais; Rossio for Sintra and the west; and Sul e Sueste for the south (including the Algarve) and the southeast (ticket prices will include ferry trip across the Tagus, if necessary).

Ferries (*barcaça*). Many boats offer services across the Tagus, up various rivers, such as the Douro and the Guadiana, to the Tróia Peninsula and to the offshore islands. Ask at local tourist offices for further details.

Hitch-hiking. Hitching is easy, if not very fast. It is illegal on motorways, and women should not travel alone. If you are travelling from the UK, contact Freewheelers (tel. (0171) 738 6861), an organisation that brings drivers and passengers together, for a small fee.

Domestic Flights. TAP (Air Portugal) flies between Lisbon, Oporto and Faro. TAP also flies from Lisbon to Madeira and the Azores: contact TAP, Praça Marquês de Pombal 3-A, Lisbon for information; for tickets; tel. (01) 386 40 80, fax (01) 386 09 30; for flight reservations; tel. (01) 841 69 90, fax (01) 841 65 40.

How much is the fare to...?	**Quanto custo o bilhete para...?**
Will you tell me when to get off?	**Pode dizer-me quando devo descer?**
Where's the nearest bus/tram stop?	**Onde fica a mais próxima paragem dos autocarros/eléctricos?**
Where can I get a taxi?	**Onde posso encontrar um táxi?**
Can you give us a lift to...?	**Pode levar-nos a...?**

TRAVELLERS WITH DISABILITIES

Portuguese tourist establishments are in the process of making sites more accessible for wheelchairs, but few places have facilities yet. Some hotels, notably the state-run pousadas (see ACCOMMODATION on p.144), have made an effort to fit out special hotel rooms. The Portuguese National Tourist Office can provide a list of hotels which are accessible, and local tourist offices will also help. *Holiday Travel Abroad*, published by RADAR, 25 Mortimer Street, London W1N 8AB, UK; tel. (0171) 637 5400, provides a list of wheelchair-accessible hotels and campsites in Portugal. You can also contact the Holiday Care Service; tel. (01293) 77 45 35, with specific enquiries.

All three airports are accessible to wheelchair users, but public transport on the whole is dated and not so easily negotiated. The National Rehabilitation Secretariat, Avenida Conde Valbom 63, 1000 Lisbon, publishes a guide to transport facilities (in Portuguese) and an *Access Guide* to Lisbon with symbols explained in English. You can rent cars with hand controls from ARAC, Rua Dr António Candido 9, 1097 Lisbon; tel. (01) 56 38 36, but they must be booked well in advance of your visit. The Dutch organisation, IHD International, Marconistraat 3, 6716 AK Ede, Netherlands, runs a wheelchair-accessible bus from Faro airport to Albufeira and Vilamoura, as well as providing other services for disabled holidaymakers.

TRAVELLING TO PORTUGAL

By Air

From the UK and Ireland: There are regular scheduled and charter flights from most British and Irish airports to all three of Portugal's international airports (see AIRPORTS on p.151). Package deals and fly-drive holidays often offer the best prices. Besides the various travel agencies, the Portuguese National Airline, TAP (Air Portugal), offers packages and competitively priced scheduled flights from Heathrow and Gatwick to Lisbon, Faro and Oporto. Contact: TAP, 38-44 Gillingham Street, 4th floor, Gillingham House, London SW1V 1HU; tel. (0171) 630 0900, fax (0171) 233 7968.

From North America and elsewhere: Portugal is on many scheduled routes from North America (New York, Boston, Los Angeles, Montreal, Toronto), and there are frequent flights from former colonies in South America and southern Africa. TAP offers a service from New York/Newark; TAP, 399 Market Street, Newark, NJ; tel. (201) 344 4490 (tickets), (800) 221 7370 (reservations).

By Road

You can drive to Portugal from other parts of continental Europe. One popular route is via France and Spain, across the western Pyrenees, and through Madrid to Portugal. There are many other access routes between Spain and Portugal.

By Rail

There are two main European routes to Lisbon (both of which take about 24 hours). One starts from Paris and goes via Hendaye, Fuentes de Onoro and Vilar Formoso; the other goes from Madrid via Valencia de Alcántara. From the UK, there are frequent trains to Paris from London (Waterloo International).

By Bus

Eurolines (52 Grosvenor Gardens, London SW1V 0AV; tel. (0171) 730 8235) runs buses from London's Victoria Station, through France and Spain, to Portugal.

By Sea

Car ferries from Plymouth or Portsmouth serve the northern Spanish ports of Santander and Bilbao, from where it is a relatively short drive to Portugal. Ferry places must be booked well ahead in the peak travel season. Some cruise ships stop in Lisbon and Oporto; check with your travel agent.

VIDEO

Standard and camcorder videotape is available, but note that European equipment is not compatible with that used in the US. Camcorders can be rented in the tourist areas.

WATER (*água*)

Tap water in Portugal is safe to drink, unless it is signposted to the contrary. Many brands of locally bottled water are available. If you want fizzy water ask for *água mineral com gás* or, if you prefer still ask for *água mineral sem gás*.

a bottle of mineral water **uma garrafa de água mineral**

Portugal

WEIGHTS and MEASURES (For fuel and distance charts see
DRIVING IN PORTUGAL on p.157)
The metric system is used in Portugal.

Length

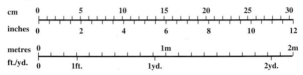

Weight

Temperature

WOMEN TRAVELLERS
Many women in Portugal relish their traditional family role, and are
offended by what they consider to be the loose behaviour of more
independent-minded women. Portugal is very safe for women, but
always take care in cities at night. IDM (Informação, Documatação
Mulheres), Rua Filipe de Mata 115A, Lisbon; tel. (01) 72 05 98, is a
women's group (with English-speaking members) that organizes
meetings, publishes a newsletter, and runs a library and café.

Y

YOUTH HOSTELS (*pousadas de juventude*)
There are 18 hostels spread across the country, many of which serve
meals. It is best to join the International Youth Hostel Federation before you depart, but you can join up on arrival as a junior member
(14 to 21 years old) or a senior (22 to 40); Associação Portuguesa de
Pousadas de Juventude (Movijovem), Avenida Duque d'Ávila 137,
1000 Lisbon; tel. (01) 355 90 81.

A SELECTION
OF HOTELS
AND RESTAURANTS

Recommended Hotels

Accommodation ranges from hotels and modern self-catering apartments to country houses (many of which belong to the Turismo de Habitação (Turihab) scheme) and converted historical buildings (Pousadas). (See ACCOMMODATION on p.150)

The hotels listed below are divided into geographical areas, then listed alphabetically. You can often get cheaper rates if your accommodation is booked as part of a package, or during the low season. The price brackets are for a double room in high season, including service, breakfast and tax.

✪✪✪✪	over 35,000 esc
✪✪✪	20,000 to 35,000 esc
✪✪	12,000 to 20,000 esc
✪	below 12,000 esc

MINHO

Casa de Rodas ✪✪ *Lugar de Rodas, 4950 Monção; Tel. (051) 65 21 05; Fax (058) 74 14 44 (Turihab).* Four rooms and one apartment in an old house on a vineyard estate.

Casa do Outeiro ✪✪ Lugar do Outeiro, 4990 Ponte de Lima; *Tel. (058) 94 12 06; Fax (058) 74 14 44 (Turihab).* Three rooms and one apartment in a traditional Minho-style farmhouse. Beamed roof, stone fireplaces, and an excellent library of books about the area. Water is supplied by an old aqueduct.

Hotel do Elevador ✪-✪✪ *Bom Jesus do Monte, 4700 Braga; Tel. (053) 67 66 11; Fax (053) 67 66 79.* Situated at the top of the funicular railway which leads to the pilgrimage church of Bom Jesus, this cool location affords a wonderful view over the Braga plain. Recently renovated. 25 rooms.

Paço de Calheiros ✪✪ *Calheiros, 4990 Ponte de Lima; Tel. (058) 94 71 64; Fax (058) 74 14 44 (Turihab).* This is probably the most sumptuous property in the Turismo de Habitação (Turihab) scheme. Located 7km (4 miles) from Ponte de Lima, the palace of the Count de Calheiros is set in terraced fields above the river. All nine rooms and six apartments are beautifully furnished. Horse riding, tennis and swimming pool.

Pinhal ✪✪ *Avenida da Praia, Ofir, 4740 Esposende; Tel. (053) 98 14 73; Fax (053) 98 22 65.* Resort hotel close to the beach. Swimming pool, tennis, horse-riding, fishing, disco. 90 rooms.

Pousada de Nossa Senhora de Oliveira ✪✪✪ *Largo da Oliveira, 4801 Guimarães; Tel. (053) 51 41 57/8/9; Fax (053) 51 42 04.* Converted 16th and 17th-century townhouses, overlooking central Guimarães. Excellent restaurant (see p.188), 16 rooms.

Pousada de Santa Marinha ✪✪✪ *Costa, 4800 Guimarães; Tel. (053) 51 44 53/4/5; Fax (053) 51 44 59.* A stunningly converted 12th-century monastery, in the Penha hills 3km (2 miles) from Guimarães. Beautiful furniture and art in the public rooms, spectacular cloister and gardens. 51 rooms.

Pousada de São Bento ✪✪✪ *4850 Caniçada; Tel. (053) 64 71 90/1; Fax (053) 64 78 67.* Converted hunting lodge in the beautiful Peneda-Gerês National Park. Great view over the dam. Excellent hiking. Swimming pool and tennis. 29 rooms.

Quinta do Convento da Franqueira ✪✪ *Franqueira, 4750 Barcelos; Tel. (053) 83 16 06; Fax (053) 81 30 61.* This hilltop Turismo de Habitação only has three rooms in a converted 16th-century convent, situated 5km (3 miles) outside the town of Barcelos and is surrounded by trees, beautiful gardens and vineyards. Swimming pool.

Santa Luzia Hotel ✪✪ *Santa Luzia, 4900 Viana do Castelo; Tel. (058) 82 88 90/1; Fax (058) 82 88 92.* A classic 1930s hotel perched on a hill and overlooking the town of Viana, the Santa Luzia pilgrimage church, the River Lima and the Atlantic. Run by ENATUR (the pousada organization), the hotel is situated next to a prehistoric *citânia* site. Tennis, swimming pool, gardens. 55 rooms.

OPORTO AND THE DOURO

Casa de Santo António de Britiande ✪✪ *Britiande, 5100 Lamego; Tel. (054) 69 93 46; Fax (054) 69 93 46;* Four rooms and one apartment in a scenic country house. Turihab member. Tennis and pool.

Hotel da Bolsa ✪-✪✪ *Rua Ferreira Borges 101, 4100 Oporto; Tel. (02) 202 67 68/69/70; Fax (02) 31 88 88.* Central location, next to the Stock Exchange. 36 rooms (one room is for disabled guests).

Ibis ✪ *Lugar das Chas-Afurada, Vila Nova de Gaia, 4400 Oporto. Tel. (02) 772 07 72; Fax (02) 772 07 88.* New, modern hotel, near the highway. Restaurant. 108 rooms.

Pousada de São Gonçalo ✪✪ *4600 Amarante; Tel. (055) 46 11 13/23/24; Fax (055) 46 13 53.* A quiet, modern pousada located in the Serra do Marão mountains, 20km (12 miles) east of Amarante. Excellent restaurant (see p.188). 15 rooms.

Quinta do Paço ✪✪ *Vila Marim, 5040 Mesão Frio; Tel. (054) 992 03/69 93 46; Fax (054) 69 93 46.* Four rooms in a large Douro manor house. Rooms for rent May to October, or you can rent the entire house at any time of the year.

Sheraton Porto ✪✪✪ *Avenida da Boavista 1269, 4100 Oporto; Tel. (02) 606 88 22; Fax (02) 609 14 67.* Situated in the western part of Oporto. Health club, indoor pool, squash, sauna. 253 rooms.

Vermar ✪✪ *Rua de Martin Vaz N-O, 4490 Póvoa de Varzim; Tel. (052) 61 55 66; Fax (052) 61 51 15.* A beachside block. Health club, pool, tennis, disco. 208 rooms.

TRÁS-OS-MONTES

Aquae Flaviae ✪✪ *Praça do Brasil, 5400 Chaves; Tel. (076) 267 11; Fax (076) 264 97.* Large new hotel with 170 rooms. Excellent facilities include six restaurants, a tennis court, five-a-side football, two small pools, gym, sauna and conference rooms. A tunnel to the spa is planned.

Casa da Avó ✪✪ *Rua de Manuel de Seixas 12, 5160 Moncorvo; Tel. (079) 224 01; fax (058) 74 14 44 (Turihab Central).* Five rooms in a 19th-century house in central Torre de Moncorvo. Closed December and January.

Casa das Quartas ✪✪ *Abrambes, 5000 Vila Real; Tel. (059) 32 29 76; Fax (059) 32 29 76.* Four rooms (three in winter) in a cosy country house just outside Vila Real. Turihab member.

Mira Corgo Hotel ✪ *Avenida 1 de Mayo 76, 5000 Vila Real; Tel. (059) 32 50 01; no fax.* High-rise hotel overlooking the Corgo gorge. Indoor pool, private garage, health club, disco. 76 rooms. No restaurant.

Moinho do Caniço ✪ *Ponte de Castrelos, Castrelos, 5300 Bragança. Tel. (073) 235 77/259 52; no fax.* This rustic former watermill on the River Baceiro, 12km (7 miles) from Bragança, has two rooms. Trout fishing available.

Pousada de Santa Catarina ✪✪ *5210 Miranda do Douro; Tel. (073) 410 05/255; Fax (073) 410 65.* A comfortable 12-room pousada overlooking the spectacular Douro gorge, dam, and Spanish border. Notable restaurant (see p.189).

Pousada de São Bartolomeu ✪✪ *5300 Bragança; Tel. (073) 33 14 93; Fax (073) 234 53.* A comfortable modern pousada overlooking the fortress and city across a small river. Good base for exploring the region. Fine regional cooking (see p.189). 16 rooms.

THE BEIRAS

Astória ✪✪ *Avenida Emídia Navarro 21, 3000 Coimbra; Tel. (039) 220 55/6; Fax (039) 220 57.* Elegant 1920s hotel, recently renovated. Free use of sports facilities at Palace Hotel da Curia (23km/14 miles away). All 64 rooms overlook the Mondego river. Notable restaurant (see p.189).

Casa da Azenha Velha ✪✪ *Caceira de Cima, 3080; Figueira da Foz; Tel. (033) 250 41/239 04; no fax.* Six rooms in a modern country house on a 12-hectare (30-acre) estate, located 9km (6 miles) from Figueira. Riding ring, tennis, pool, great for walks.

Dom João III ✪✪ *Avenida Heróis de Angola, 2400 Leiria; Tel. (044) 81 25 00; Fax (044) 81 22 35.* Functional 64-room hotel, part of the Best Western chain. Private garage. Scenic views of castle.

Grão Vasco ✪✪ *Rua Gaspar Barreiros, 3500 Viseu; Tel. (032) 42 35 11/2/3; Fax (032) 42 64 44.* This 112-room hotel has fine public rooms, an outdoor pool, gardens and an Avis car-rental office. Close to the centre of town.

Imperial ✪✪ *Rua Dr Nascimento Leitão, 3800 Aveiro; Tel. (034) 221 41; Fax (034) 241 48.* Modern and efficient 107-room hotel, with views over the lagoon from the terrace.

Palace Hotel do Buçaco ✪✪✪ *Buçaco, 3050 Mealhada; Tel. (031) 93 01 01; Fax (031) 93 05 09.* Wonderfully grand and palatial hotel, set in the Buçaco forest. Splendid decoration and public rooms. Good restaurant. Fine gardens, tennis. 60 rooms.

Pousada do Mestre Afonso Domingues ✪✪ *2440 Batalha; Tel. (044) 962 60/1; Fax (044) 962 47.* Relaxed new 21-room pousada, located on the plaza surrounding the Batalha monastery and named after the monastery's first architect. Good restaurant (see p.189).

Rainha Dona Amélia ✪✪ *Rua de Santiago 15, 6000 Castelo Branco; Tel. (072) 32 63 15; Fax (072) 32 63 90.* Pleasant 64-room modern hotel close to the historic centre.

Tivoli ✪✪-✪✪✪ *Rua João Machado, 3000 Coimbra; Tel. (039) 269 34, Fax (039) 268 27.* The Tivoli is a very efficient, modern, 94-room hotel, with a health club, private garage, and good conference facilities.

Turismo ✪✪ *Avenida Coronel O de Carvalho, 6300 Guarda; Tel. (071) 21 22 05; Fax (071) 21 22 04.* Pleasant modern 106-room hotel on the outskirts of the city. Popular with business travellers.

ESTREMADURA AND RIBATEJO

Casa da Pérgola ✪✪ *Avenida de Valbom 13, 2750 Cascais; Tel. (01) 484 00 40; no fax.* Central location. Elegant mansion with 10 rooms. Open March to October. Turihab member.

Estalagem de Santa Iria ✪✪ *Mouchão Parque, 2300 Tomar; Tel. (049) 31 33 26/32 12 38; Fax (049) 32 10 82.* Scenic inn in a quiet park on a river island. Restaurant housed in a medieval-style hall. 13 rooms.

Palácio ✪✪✪✪ *Rua do Parque, 2765 Estoril; Tel. (01) 468 04 00; Fax (01) 468 48 67.* Stylish 1930s luxury hotel facing the casino gardens. Six tennis courts, pool, special rates for golf enthusiasts at Estoril Golf Club. The hotel's Four Seasons restaurant is excellent. 162 rooms.

Palácio de Seteais ✪✪✪✪ *Rua Barbosa do Bocage, 2710 Sintra; Tel. (01) 923 32 00; Fax (01) 923 42 77.* The Palácio de Seteais is a luxurious 18th-century palace elegantly furnished with antiques and fine pieces of reproduction furniture. Wonderful views, heated outdoor pool, tennis. 30 rooms.

Pousada de Palmela ✪✪✪ *2950 Palmela; Tel. (01) 235 12 26/235 13 95; Fax (01) 233 04 40.* A luxurious bright-white hilltop pousada that has been a fortress, a monastery and a mosque. The dining room is in the old monks' refectory. 28 rooms.

Pousada do Castelo ✪✪✪ *2510 Óbidos; Tel. (062) 95 91 05/46; Fax (062) 95 91 48.* One of Portugal's most luxurious pousadas, located within the castle walls of a 15th-century royal palace, which itself forms part of the town walls. Excellent restaurant. Nine rooms.

Quinta de Vale de Lobos ✪✪ *2000 Santarém; Tel. (043) 42 92 64; Fax (043) 42 93 13.* Four rooms in a 19th-century farmhouse and two bungalows set in a 243-hectare (600-acre) estate, 6km (3 miles) north of Santarém, once the home of the liberal politician Alexandre Herculano. Swimming pool, hunting.

Quinta do Campo ✪✪ *Valado dos Frades, 2450 Nazaré; Tel. (062) 57 71 35/26/68; Fax (062) 57 75 55.* This estate was formerly a Cistercian agricultural school. The charming manor house is located close to a pine forest, 6km (3 miles) outside Nazaré. Pool, tennis, 10 rooms. Meals on request.

Vilazul ✪✪ *Calçada de Baleia 10, 2655 Ericeira. Tel. (061) 86 41 01; Fax (061) 629 27.* This central family-run establishment has 21 small but bright rooms, and the top floor has balconies with views of the sea. The Restaurant Poço, downstairs, is worth a visit (see p.190). There is a rooftop bar and an English-style pub in the basement.

LISBON

Eduardo VII ✪✪✪ *Avenida Fontes Pereira de Melo 5, 1000 Lisbon; Tel. (01) 353 01 41; Fax (01) 353 38 79.* Classic old hotel overlooking Eduardo VII park. Recently redecorated. There is a rooftop restaurant with great views over the capital city. 121 rooms.

Hotel da Lapa ✪✪✪✪ *Rua do Pau de Bandeira 4, 1200 Lisbon; Tel. (01) 395 00 05; Fax (01) 395 06 65.* Beautifully restored 19th-century palace in the stylish embassy district. The restaurant serves excellent French-Portuguese style fare. Scenic garden, indoor and outdoor swimming pools. 102 rooms and eight apartments.

Portugal

Lisboa Penta ✪✪✪ *Avenida dos Combatentes, 1600 Lisbon; Tel. (01) 726 40 54; Fax (01) 726 42 81.* The Lisboa Penta is a massive 588-room hotel near the Gulbenkian Museum, geared towards business congresses. Health club, outdoor pool, shopping gallery, shuttle bus to centre.

Lutécia ✪✪✪ *Avenida Frei Miguel Contreiras 52, 1700 Lisbon; Tel. (01) 80 31 21; Fax (01) 80 78 18.* Modern 151-room hotel with good access to the airport.

Miraparque ✪✪ *Avenida Sidónio Pais 12, 1000 Lisbon; Tel. (01) 57 80 70; Fax (01) 57 89 20.* Pleasant hotel with 108 rooms overlooking Eduardo VII park, conveniently located near Pombal.

Quinta Nova da Conceição ✪✪ *Rua da Cidade de Rabat 5, 1500 Lisbon; Tel. (01) 778 00 91; Fax (01) 778 00 91.* Three rooms in this rare example of an urban Turismo de Habitação, an 18th-century townhouse surrounded by a garden. Breakfast only. Closed August.

Ritz InterContinental ✪✪✪✪ *Rua Rodrigo da Fonseca 88, 1093 Lisbon; Tel. (01) 69 20 20; Fax (01) 69 17 83.* Well-appointed luxury hotel with 310 rooms and several suites that have been decorated by artists. All rooms have a large private balcony. Sixth floor reserved for non-smokers. Shopping gallery.

York House ✪✪✪ *Rua das Janelas Verdes 32, 1200 Lisbon; Tel. (01) 396 25 44; Fax (01) 397 27 93.* Located in a 16th-century convent near the Museum of Ancient Art – one of the most charming areas in Lisbon. The 35 rooms are beautifully furnished and set around a fine courtyard.

ALENTEJO

Casa das Janelas Verdes ✪ *Rua Dr Manuel Francisco Gomes 38-40, 7750 Mértola; Tel. (086) 621 45; no fax.* Three rooms set in a traditional house in the centre of the old town, with a courtyard and fruit trees. Good location for fishing and hunting. Closed between July and August.

Casa de Peixinhos ✪ *7160 Vila Viçosa; Tel. (068) 984*

72/988 59; no fax. Six rooms in an old 17th-century manor house surrounded by orange trees, 500m (⅓mile) from town. Closed during late December and August.

Herdade do Topo ✪✪✪ *Monte do Topo, PO Box 29, 7830 Serpa; Tel. (084) 591 36; Fax (084) 592 60.* Four rooms on a working stud farm, 12km (7 miles) from Serpa. Specializes in equestrian tourism. For an all-in price you get full board, open bar, daily horse-riding lesson, use of the horses and a round of clay-pigeon shooting.

Pousada de Santa Luzia ✪✪ *Avenida de Badajoz, 7350 Elvas; Tel. (068) 62 21 94/62 21 28; Fax (068) 62 21 27.* Portugal's first pousada, near to the fortress of Elvas. Good stopping off point to or from Spain. Notable restaurant. 25 rooms.

Pousada de São Fransisco ✪✪✪. *Largo D Nuno Álvares Pereira, 7800 Beja; Tel. (084) 32 84 41; Fax (084) 32 91 43.* This newly-opened pousada has 35 rooms in a wonderfully converted convent. The large barrel-vaulted church is used for conferences and the chapterhouse as a bar. One room is especially equipped for disabled guests. Tennis and outdoor pool.

Pousada de São Gens ✪✪ *7830 Serpa; Tel. (084) 537 24/5; Fax (084) 533 37.* Modern pousada with great views, situated outside Serpa. Swimming pool. 18 rooms.

Pousada de São Tiago ✪✪ *Estrada de Lisboa, 7540 Santiago do Cacém; Tel. (069) 224 59; Fax (069) 224 59.* Comfortable small country house with eight rooms, close to the Miróbriga ruins. Swimming pool.

Pousada dos Lóios ✪✪✪ *Largo Conde de Vila Flor, 7000 Évora; Tel. (066) 240 51/2; Fax (066) 272 48.* Luxurious 32-room pousada in a 15th-century convent, located next to a Roman temple. Restaurant in a cloister (see p.192). Restored chapel. Outdoor pool.

Santa Clara ✪ *Travessa da Milheira 19, 7000 Évora; Tel. (066) 241 41/2; Fax (066) 265 44.* Functional but central hotel in quiet side street, with 43 rooms. Restaurant open in high season only (breakfast all year).

ALGARVE

Bela Vista ✪✪✪ *Avenida Tomás Cabreira, Praia da Rocha, 8500 Portimão. Tel. (082) 240 55; Fax (082) 41 53 69.* A beautiful inn, with 14 rooms, located near the beach in a summer mansion, with splendid wooden ceilings and *azulejos*.

Estalagem Aeromar ✪✪ *Praia de Faro, 8000 Faro; Tel. (089) 81 71 89/81 75 42; Fax (089) 81 75 12.* Right on the town beach and close to the airport, with 23 rooms and a good grill restaurant.

Eva ✪✪ *Avenida da República, 8000 Faro; Tel. (089) 80 55 54; Fax (089) 80 23 04.* Modern 150-room tower block, overlooking the marina, right in the centre of town. Disco and swimming pool.

Golfinho ✪✪✪ *Praia Dona Ana, 8600 Lagos; Tel. (082) 76 99 00; Fax (082) 76 99 20.* An eight-storey block, with 262 rooms, above Dona Ana beach. Indoor and outdoor pools, disco, bowling alley. Disabled access.

Loulé Jardim ✪ *Praça Manuel de Arriaga, 8100 Loulé; Tel. (089) 41 30 94; Fax (089) 63 177;* Pretty location, 10km (6 miles) inland. Pool. 52 rooms. There is no restaurant.

Pousada do Infante ✪✪✪ *Sítio da Baleira, 8650 Sagres; Tel. (082) 642 22/3; Fax (082) 642 25.* Modern 39-room pousada on the cliffs near the fortress. Pool and tennis. Also has an annexe in the historic Fortaleza do Belize, on the way to Cabo de São Vicente.

Quinta da Fonte do Bispo ✪ *Sítio da Fonte do Bispo - Santa Catarina, 8800 Tavira; Tel. (081) 97 14 84; no fax.* Six rooms in a country house, 11km (7 miles) from Tavira.

Sheraton Algarve ✪✪✪✪ *Praia da Falésia, 8200 Albufeira; Tel. (089) 50 19 99; Fax (089) 50 19 50.* New luxury-class 215-room hotel, above the beach, 10km (6 miles) east of Albufeira. Indoor and outdoor pools, nine-hole private golf course, tennis, health club. Lifts provided to the beach.

Recommended Restaurants

Portuguese restaurants serve large portions of hearty food, often very reasonably priced (see EATING OUT on p.135). The *ementa turística* (tourist menu) is usually good value and costs between 1,000 and 3,000 escudos.

The price bands given below are per person for a starter, main course and dessert (but not wine), including service and sales tax. The restaurants are divided into geographical areas and listed alphabetically.

✪✪✪	over 5,500 esc
✪✪	4,000-5,500 esc
✪	below 4,000 esc

MINHO

Bagoeira ✪ *Avenida Sidónio Pais 57, 4750 Barcelos; Tel. (053) 81 12 36.* The Bagoeira is a very popular local restaurant with 19th-century décor. Absolutely packed on market days. For a taste of authentic regional fare try the grilled meat and some of the local sweets, such as stuffed oranges.

Churrasqueiria Tulha ✪ *Rua Formosa, 4990 Ponte de Lima; Tel. (058) 94 28 79.* The menu at this restaurant comprises reasonably-priced grilled meat and fish, served in the setting of a converted barn. It also offers the local speciality of *sarrabulho* (minced meats and pig's blood). Very good local *vinho verde*.

Inácio ✪✪ *Campo das Hortas 4, 4700 Braga; Tel. (053) 61 32 25.* The most popular restaurant in Braga. The house speciality is the classic Minho dish of *lampreia com arroz* (a lamprey stew with rice), which is not to be missed. Closed Tuesday.

Pousada de Dom Dinis ✪✪ *4920 Vila Nova de Cerveira; Tel. (051) 79 56 01.* The Pousada de Dom Dinis is in the ruins of an ancient walled village overlooking the Minho river. There is a strong emphasis on Minhoetan cuisine.

Pousada de Nossa Senhora de Oliveira ✪✪ *Largo da Oliveira, 4801 Guimarães; Tel. (053) 51 41 57/8/9.* Located in the pousada in central Guimarães (see p.178). Very good Portuguese and international cuisine. Try the *bife especial à pousada* (châteaubriand).

OPORTO AND THE DOURO

Dom Tonho ✪✪ *Cais da Ribeira 13-15, 4000 Oporto; Tel. (02) 200 43 07.* Beautifully located in an old townhouse on the riverfront. The Dom Tonho specialises in seafood as well as local dishes, but sometimes mounts theme weeks during which the restaurant features foods from different regions in Portugal, such as the Minho or the Azores.

O Marinheiro ✪✪ *Estrada N13, A Ver-o-Mar, 4490 Póvoa de Varzim; Tel. (052) 68 21 51.* For those in search of a truly nautical place to eat, the O Marinheiro has been made up to look like a beached fishing boat. Tanks filled with fish and shellfish provide the main ingredient for your meal.

Portucale ✪✪✪ *Rua da Alegria 598, 4000 Oporto; Tel. (02) 57 07 17.* Excellent restaurant set on top of a large building with one of the best views in the city. The menu is a mix of French and Portuguese dishes, including lobster thermidor and Oporto-style tripe.

Pousada de São Gonçalo ✪ *4600 Amarante; Tel. (055) 46 11 13/23/24.* Set in a scenic mountain pousada (see p.179). Local dishes include Serrana-style kid stew, and trout stuffed with smoked ham.

Varanda da Régua ✪ *Peso da Régua; Tel. (054) 247 49.* Good regional food with a great view of the Douro, 8km (5 miles) out of town on the Loureiro road.

TRÁS-OS-MONTES

Dionizyos ✪ *Praça do Muncípio 2, 5400 Chaves; Tel. (076) 237 51.* Centrally located by the castle, this place will fill you up with cheap, hearty fare. Try *folar* (a local pork bread).

Espadeiro ✪ *Avenida Almeida Lucena, 5000 Vila Real; Tel. (059) 32 23 02.* Considered the best restaurant in Vila Real. Serves regional dishes in comfortable surroundings.

Poças ✪ *Rua Combatentes da Grande Guerra 200, 5300 Bragança. Tel. (073) 224 28.* Poças is a very popular local hangout serving regional food in traditionally huge portions. Try the interesting *alheira* sausage, made with turkey in place of pork by Jews who had been forced to convert to Christianity.

Pousada de Santa Catarina ✪-✪✪ *5210 Miranda do Douro; Tel. (073) 410 05/255.* This pousada restaurant overlooks the Douro gorge (see p.180). A local favourite is an enormous slab of braised steak (*posta à Mirandesa*). Spanish pesetas are also accepted here.

Pousada de São Bartolomeu ✪-✪✪ *5300 Bragança; Tel. (073) 33 14 93.* The restaurant in this pousada (see p.180) overlooks the city. Its menu emphasises the cooking of Trás-os-Montes region with a variety of classic dishes such as *polvo à Transmontana* (octopus cooked in its own ink) and trout wrapped in cured ham.

THE BEIRAS

L'Amphitryon ✪✪ *Hotel Astória, Avenida Emídia Navarro 21, 3000 Coimbra. Tel. (039) 220 55.* Elegant restaurant in the Hotel Astória (see p.181), serving Portuguese and French cuisine. Good selection of Buçaco wines.

O Cortiço ✪-✪✪ *Rua Augusto Hilário 47, 3500 Viseu; Tel. (032) 42 38 53.* Friendly *típico* in the historic centre, with restaurants on both sides of the street. Local food, mainly meat. Try the interestingly named 'Duck roasted by Miss Cilinha from Viseu'.

Estrela do Mar ✪ *Travessa da Rua Direita 7, 3800 Aveiro; Tel. (034) 203 92.* Functional restaurant serving local lagoon fish prepared in a Cantonese style.

Pousada do Mestre Afonso Domingues ✪✪ *2440*

Batalha; Tel. (044) 96 260/1. Pousada restaurant (see p.181) located adjacent to the famous monastery. Serves regional specialities such as farmhands' soup and *bacalhau à d'Álvares.*

Praça Velha ✪ *Largo Luis de Camões 17, 6000 Castelo Branco; Tel. (072) 32 86 40.* In a 17th-century house in the old town, this restaurant serves regional specialities, such as roast kid, and goats' cheese.

ESTREMADURA AND RIBATEJO

Arte Xavega ✪✪ *Calçada do Sítio, 2450 Nazaré; Tel. (062) 55 21 36.* In the Sítio district, up the funicular railway. Serves both Portuguese and international cuisine. Try a *caldeirada* (seafood stew).

Bela Vista ✪ *Rua Fonte do Choupo 6, 2300 Tomar; Tel. (049) 31 28 70.* You can't go far wrong at the Bela Vista – considered the best choice in town. Great views of historic Tomar. Eat outdoors in summer. Try the *frango à caril* (curried chicken). The restaurant is closed on Monday evening, Tuesday, and in November.

Cozinha Velha ✪✪ *Palácio de Queluz, 2745 Queluz; Tel. (01) 435 02 32.* Excellent restaurant in the 'Pink Palace' of Queluz. You can dine on 18th-century style meals in the old kitchen or in the splendid Sala Dourada (Golden Room). The restaurant is run by the pousada organisation, ENATUR.

Poço ✪ *Hotel Vilazul, Calçada de Baleia 10, 2655 Ericeira; Tel. (061) 86 41 01.* Popular local seafood restaurant in the Hotel Vilazul (see p.183). Make sure you try the local speciality, *açorda de marisco.*

Solar de São Pedro ✪✪ *Praça Dom Fernando II 12, 2710 São Pedro de Sintra; Tel. (01) 923 18 60.* French restaurant serving *coxas de rã à Provençal* (frogs' legs). The steaks are recommended. Closed on Wednesday.

LISBON

Arcadas do Faia ✪✪✪ *Rua da Barroca 56, 1200 Lisbon; Tel. (01) 342 67 42.* The Arcadas do Faia is set in a classic Bairro Alto *fado* house. Closed on Sunday.

O Cardo ✪ *Avenida Fontes Pereira de Melo, 3-C, 1000 Lisbon; Tel. (01) 53 82 94.* This friendly, inexpensive restaurant sports fish tanks in its window and serves excellent seafood, as well as several other classic Portuguese dishes.

Casa de Pasto Alentejana ✪ *2 Praçeta Goa, 1200 Lisbon; Tel. (01) 921 97 17.* In a fascinating old building, decorated with *azulejos*, near Restauradores. Popular with Alentejanos living in Lisbon. Large portions served cheaply at the bar. Casual.

Casa do Leão ✪✪✪ *Castelo de São Jorge, 1100 Lisbon; Tel. (01) 87 59 62.* You will find the Casa do Leão inside the São Jorge Castle, with its vaulted brick ceiling. Run by ENATUR (the pousada organisation). Serves both regional dishes and international cuisine.

Gambrinus ✪✪✪ *Rua das Portas de Santo Antão 25, 1100 Lisbon; Tel. (01) 342 14 66.* Central restaurant specialising in regional seafood dishes. Try the *ameijoas à bulhão pato* (steamed clams with garlic and coriander). Excellent service.

ALENTEJO

Adega do Isaías ✪ *Rua do Almeida 21, 7100 Estremoz; Tel. (068) 233 18.* The Adega do Isaías is an atmospheric old wine cellar serving excellent pork and lamb cooked in the Alentejo style.

Alentejano ✪ *Praça da República, 7830 Serpa; Tel. (084) 533 35.* Friendly family restaurant upstairs and busier café downstairs. Very good dishes from the Alentejo, especially soups and stews highly flavoured with garlic and coriander. The local goats' cheese is also very good.

Portugal

Cozinha de Santo Humberto ✪✪ *Rua da Moeda 39, 7000 Évora; Tel. (066) 242 51.* Highly recommended restaurant in an ancient cellar. Serves all the classic dishes of the Alentejo and is strong on game dishes, such as wild boar or partridge.

Pousada dos Lóios ✪✪ *Largo Conde de Vila Flor, 7000 Évora; Tel. (066) 240 51/2.* Beautifully located in the cloister of an old monastery, now a pousada (see p.185). Serves a selection of regional Alentejano cuisine and Portuguese dishes.

O Virgilio ✪ *Rua dos Infantes, 7800 Beja; Tel. (084) 257 50* Small, cheery restaurant serving traditional Alentejano dishes.

ALGARVE

O Caneção ✪ *Rua José Pires Padinha 162, 8800 Tavira; Tel. (081) 819 21.* On the quayside and specialising in fresh seafood. Local favourites are *atum* (tuna) and *cataplana de tamboril* (a seafood stew made with monkfish).

Dois Irmãos ✪✪ *Largo do Terreiro do Bispo 18, 8000 Faro; Tel. (089) 233 37.* Long-established fish restaurant, the 'Two Brothers' serves regional dishes, including no less than nine varieties of *cataplana*.

Dom Henrique ✪✪ *Rua 25 de Abril 75, 8600 Lagos; Tel. (082) 76 35 63.* Formal restaurant serving Portuguese and international cuisine. In the centre of the old town. Good seafood dishes.

Jardim d'Allah ✪✪ *Beco José Bernadino de Souza, 8200 Albufeira; Tel. (089) 51 32 29.* Reflecting the Algarve's previous incarnation as the Moorish Kingdom of al-Gharb, this restaurant serves North African dishes.

Rui Marisqeiria ✪ *Albergaria Solar da Moura, 8300 Silves; Tel. (082) 44 31 06.* Seafood restaurant in the Albergaria Solar da Moura. Especially good for shellfish.

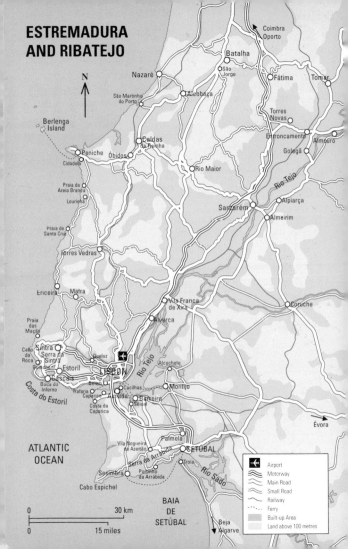

ESTREMADURA
AND RIBATEJO

Coimbra
Oporto

Batalha

São Jorge

Nazaré

Fátima

Tomar

Alcobaça

São Martinho
do Porto

Torres
Novas

N

Berlenga
Island

Caldas
da Rainha

Entroncamento

Almourol

Golegã

Peniche

Óbidos

Cidadela

Rio Maior

Rio Tejo

Praia da
Areia Branca

Alpiarça

Santarém

Lourinhã

Almeirim

Praia de
Santa Cruz

Torres Vedras

Ericeira

Mafra

Vila Franca
de Xira

Coruche

Praia
das
Maçãs

Alverca

Cabo
da
Roca

Sintra
Serra de
Sintra

Queluz

Alcochete

Guincho

Estoril

LISBON

Rio Tejo

Cascais

Belém

Doca do
Inferno

Trafaria
Caparica

Cacilhas

Montijo

Barreiro

Costa da
Caparica

Almada

Seixal

Costa do Estoril

ATLANTIC
OCEAN

Vila Nogueira
de Azeitão

Palmela

Évora

SETÚBAL

Serra da Arrábida

Rio Sado

Sesimbra

Portinho
da Arrábida

Tróia

Cabo Espichel

✈	Airport
〜	Motorway
〜	Main Road
〜	Small Road
〜	Railway
····	Ferry
	Built-up Area
	Land above 100 metres

0 ——— 30 km

0 ——— 15 miles

BAIA
DE
SETÚBAL

Beja
Algarve

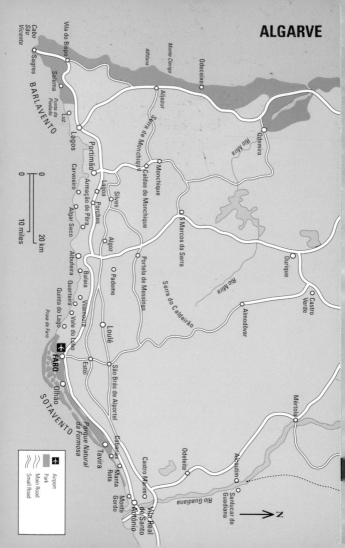

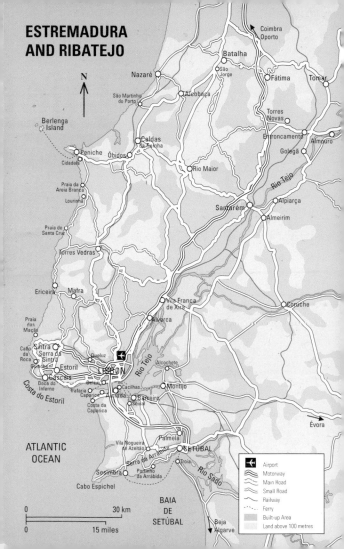

ESTREMADURA
AND RIBATEJO

N

Coimbra
Oporto

Batalha

São Jorge

Nazaré

Fátima

Tomar

Alcobaça

São Martinho
do Porto

Torres
Novas

Berlenga
Island

Entroncamento

Caldas
da Rainha

Peniche
Cidadela

Almourol

Óbidos

Golegã

Rio Maior

Praia da
Areia Branca

Rio Tejo

Lourinhã

Santarém

Alpiarça

Praia de
Santa Cruz

Almeirim

Torres Vedras

Ericeira

Mafra

Vila Franca
de Xira

Coruche

Praia das
Maçãs

Alverca

Cabo
da Roca

Sintra
Serra de
Sintra

Queluz

Guincho

Estoril

Alcochete

LISBON

Cascais

Belém

Rio Tejo

Doca do
Inferno

Cacilhas

Évora

Trafaria

Montijo

Barreiro

Costa da
Estoril

Costa da
Caparica

Almada

Seixal

ATLANTIC
OCEAN

Vila Nogueira
de Azeitão

Palmela

Serra da Arrábida

SETÚBAL

Sesimbra

Portinho
da Arrábida

Tróia

Rio Sado

Cabo Espichel

BAIA
DE
SETÚBAL

	Airport
	Motorway
	Main Road
	Small Road
	Railway
	Ferry
	Built-up Area
	Land above 100 metres

0   30 km

0   15 miles

Beja
Algarve

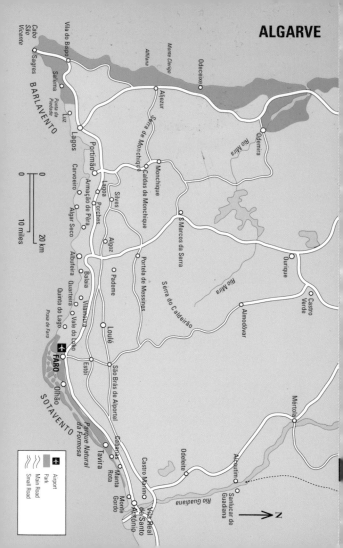

ALGARVE

BARLAVENTO

Cabo São Vicente
Sagres
Vila do Bispo
Salema
Luz
Punta da Piedade
Lagos
Portimão
Carvoeiro
Armação de Pêra
Algar Seco
Albufeira
Balaia
Quarteira
Vale do Lobo
Quinta do Lago
Praia de Faro

FARO ✈

SOTAVENTO

Parque Natural da Formosa
Olhão
Tavira
Cabanas
Manta Rota
Castro Marim
Vila Real de Santo António
Monte Gordo

Odeceixe
Aljezur
Monte Clérigo
Alfilina
Monchique
Caldas de Monchique
Serra de Monchique
Silves
Lagoa
Porches
Alpoz
Pademe
Vilamoura
Loulé
Estoi
São Brás de Alportel
Odeleite

Odemira
Rio Mira
S Marcos da Serra
Portela de Messines
Serra do Caldeirão
Rio Mira
Almodóvar

Ourique
Castro Verde
Mértola
Alcoutim
Sanlúcar de Guadiana
Rio Guadiana

0
0
10 miles
20 Km

N →

Airport
Park
Main Road
Small Road

Berlitz®

Portugal
pocket guide

The acclaimed Berlitz Pocket Guides
are packed with a world of information
Each guide is carefully researched, fu
to read, and easy to use.

Whether planning a trip to Portugal fo
business or pleasure, this guide will
help you get the most from your trip.

- Information about must-see sights,
  transportation, and emergencies

- Detailed maps and stunning
  photography

- Unique Berlitz language and culture
  tips

- Latest recommendations for hotels,
  restaurants, shopping, sports,
  festivals, and nightlife

http://www.berlitz.com

ISBN 2-8315-6316-X

9 782831 563169

US $ 10.95 UK £ 6.95

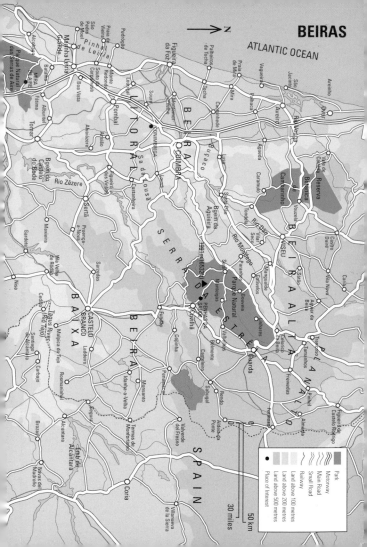